Budapest Travel Guide

BUDAPEST
TRAVEL GUIDE
(2023)

What You Should Know Before Your Trip, Great Places to Visit, Stunning Attractions, and Top Things to Do. (Essential Travel Budget Tips)

Randal E. Hernandez

Copyright

No part of this book may be reproduced in any written, electronic, recording, or photocopying without written permission of the publisher or author.

The exception would be in the case of brief quotations embodied in the critical articles or reviews and pages where permission is specifically granted by the publisher or author.

Although every precaution has been taken to verify the accuracy of the information contained herein, the author and publisher assume no responsibility for any errors or omissions. No liability is assumed for damages that may result from the use of the information contained within.

All Right Reserved©2023

Budapest Travel Guide

TABLE OF CONTENT

WELCOME TO BUDAPEST

CHAPTER 1
BUDAPEST, THE CAPITAL CITY OF HUNGARY
HISTORY OF BUDAPEST
STUNNING ATTRACTIONS IN BUDAPEST
PARKS AND RESERVES IN BUDAPEST
BUDAPEST'S BEST MUSEUMS

CHAPTER 2
BEST BEACHES IN BUDAPEST
BEST PLACES TO STAY IN BUDAPEST
TOP-RATED HOTELS IN BUDAPEST
CHEAP HOTELS IN BUDAPEST

CHAPTER 3
HOW TO MOVE AROUND IN AND AROUND BUDAPEST

CHAPTER 4
BEST SHOPPING LOCATIONS IN BUDAPEST
BEST BUDAPEST NIGHTLIFE
FUN FACTS ABOUT BUDAPEST

CHAPTERS 5

Budapest Travel Guide

TRAVELING ESSENTIALS
THE BEST OF FESTIVALS IN BUDAPEST
MONTH BY MONTH IN BUDAPEST
CHAPTER 6
ACTIVITIES DURING SUMMER
ACTIVITIES DURING SPRING
ACTIVITIES DURING WINTER
ACTIVITIES DURING AUTUMN
CHAPTER 7
SAFETY TIPS IN BUDAPEST

Budapest Travel Guide

WELCOME TO BUDAPEST

Budapest is a city that is abundant not only in terms of culture and beauty but also history. The city of Budapest, which serves as the capital of Hungary, is frequently listed among the top 10 most visited cities in the world. On the banks of the Danube River, it may be found in the middle of Europe. It should not come as a surprise that Budapest should be on everyone's travel bucket list at least once in their lifetime given the city's beautiful architecture, cuisine that is recognized around the world, and booming nightlife scene.

The Danube River physically divides the city of Budapest into two parts, which are referred to as Buda and Pest respectively. Buda is the oldest and most historically important area of the city, and it is also the home of many of the city's most noteworthy monuments, such as the Matthias Church, the Fisherman's Bastion, and the Buda Castle. Buda is the district that contains the majority of the city's most famous buildings. Pest is the area of the city that is more modern and contemporary, and it is home to some of the city's most well-known tourist locations, such as the Hungarian Parliament Building, St. Stephen's Basilica, and the Central Market Hall. Pest is also known as Pesti. In certain circles, Pest is sometimes referred to as the Pester district.

One of the most persuasive reasons in favor of everyone's inclusion of Budapest on their vacation itinerary is the city's stunning architecture. The magnificent Buda Castle and the equally breathtaking Hungarian Parliament Building are just two examples of the many breathtaking buildings that can be viewed in Budapest, which is home to some of the most breathtaking architecture in the world. Budapest is home to some of the most breathtaking architecture in the world. In addition, travelers have the option to take a stroll about the streets of the historic city, which are covered with cobblestones, and to examine the unique architecture of the city's numerous churches and cathedrals.

An additional strong reason in favor of a vacation to Budapest is that the city has a rich history and culture. The city has been there for a very long time and has a rich history, both of which may be studied by visitors at any one of the countless museums or galleries that can be found placed all across the city. In addition, Budapest plays home to a plethora of events that take place at different times throughout the year. One of these events is called the Sziget Festival, and another is called the Budapest Spring Festival. Both of these festivals provide wonderful opportunities to get a more in-depth comprehension of the vibrant culture and extensive history of this city.

The city of Budapest is especially well-known for its cuisine, and the city's many restaurants offer guests a diverse range of traditional Hungarian fare from which to choose. The guests have the option of a vast array of exquisite delights, ranging from goulash to paprikash, that is likely to thrill their senses of smell and taste. In addition, Budapest is home to a diverse selection of trendy eateries, cafes, and nightclubs. These restaurants provide their clients the unique chance to indulge in a mouthwatering dinner as well as a few refreshing drinks in a setting that is one of a kind.

Last but not least, Budapest is well-known for having a bustling atmosphere in the nightlife sector. A night out at one of the city's many clubs, bars, or pubs, where they may dance the night away to some of the greatest music available, is something that tourists might want to do while they are in town. The city is home to a large number of these establishments. In addition, Budapest is the location of a number of the most prominent music festivals in the world, such as the Balaton Sound Festival and the Volt Festival. At these festivals, visitors have the opportunity to witness some of the most outstanding examples of music from all over the world.

Budapest is a city that should be visited by every one for a variety of reasons, including the city's thriving culture and nightlife, in addition to its stunning architecture. A visit to Budapest is bound to be an experience that you won't forget because of the city's rich history, world-famous cuisine, and excellent entertainment options.

Get yourself organized, since you're going to want to take in the sights of Budapest, the magnificent capital city of Hungary.

CHAPTER 1

BUDAPEST, THE CAPITAL CITY OF HUNGARY

Budapest is a city that has always had and always will have clear socioeconomic divisions. In the past, the city displayed a deep-seated discrepancy in the way of life between the aristocrats, who constructed palaces in the town center, and those who lived in the slum districts and large temporary barrack settlements on the city's outskirts. The aristocracy built the palaces. The nobility built palaces in the central part of the town. During the Stalinist period that followed World War II, these disparities were, for the most part, eliminated; nonetheless, there has been a continuing chronic housing shortage.

Still today, the great majority of people living in the city make their lives in flats that are on the more compact side. Since the late 1960s, economic reforms have generated new wealth, which has, in turn, widened the gap between the more extravagant lifestyle of the new middle classes, whose privileged members can build second homes in the Buda Hills and on Lake Balaton, and that of the workers who populate the gigantic faceless housing estates of the drab outlying residential districts. This has increased the number of people living in poverty. In other words, the economic changes have resulted in a more conspicuous way of life for members of the emerging middle classes.

In the past, this was never the case; nevertheless, nowadays, the nation's capital is entirely Hungarian-speaking, despite the great number of visitors that come from other nations. People from an astonishing variety of racial and ethnic origins make up Budapest's population, which has proven to be one of the city's most valuable assets. In the distant past, the city of Buda was governed by German burghers and, later, by a coalition of German and Hungarian burghers. At the turn of the 19th century, the administration of Pest was administered by German burghers, the shipping sector was dominated by Serbs, and the bulk of the city's merchants identified as "Greek." (i.e., Greek and other Balkan peoples). At the same time that immigrants speaking German who worked in factories came from the West, significant numbers of Jews came from the East. They arrived in the nation at the same time. However, although close to one-quarter of Budapest's population identified as Jewish around the year 1900, the Holocaust did a substantial amount of harm to the city's Jewish community. Even though there is a small population of people from other ethnic groups in Budapest, such as Germans, Romanians, Russians, and Roma, the city as a whole has maintained its cultural homogeneity since the end of the war and has continued to do so in the early 21st century as well.

Economy Developed from early times to be the true core of the country's economy, the town was originally self-sufficient in food production when it first established itself. This occurred when it first established itself as a settlement. Before Phylloxera, which is a genus of plant louse, and urban expansion ravaged the vineyards that originally covered the upper river terraces of the Danube, Buda's wine had a well-deserved reputation for quality. Urban growth also contributed to the devastation of the vineyards. Even though the Buda Hills is home to several orchards, gardens, and nurseries in addition to dairy farms, this region only accounts for a minute percentage of the food that is now eaten in the nation's capital. The remaining territory of Hungary is in charge of supplying this food.

By the middle of the second decade of the 21st century, Budapest had developed into one of the metropolitan economies that were developing at the fastest pace anywhere in the whole world. It had grown into a notable hub of finance, banking, and commerce, in addition to being the focal point of a significant amount of direct investment from foreign sources. In addition to that, it was an important research and development facility. It should not come as a surprise that the majority of the country's prominent software companies have picked Budapest as the location of their primary operations center.

The rapid expansion of Budapest during the last several decades. It is currently the hub of the country's major thoroughfares and vital rail lines, all of which radiate from the nation's capital, which is a well-known crossing place on the Danube at which highways have traditionally converged. In addition to this, it was the company that was responsible for the development of Hungary's largest bus terminal as well as Budapest Ferenc Liszt International Airport, which is the largest commercial airport in the country. The Csepel Free Port, which is situated on Csepel Island downstream from the city center, is designed to manage container traffic and is responsible for the management of the international freight cargo that is moved on the Danube. The International Danube Commission has its main office in Budapest, which is also the capital of Hungary. The Széchenyi Chain Bridge, also known as the Széchenyi Lánchd, is the most well-known and the oldest of the city's eight bridges. It was built in the 1840s and was given its current name in honor of István Széchenyi, a Hungarian reformer who flourished in the 19th century.

To reach the summit of János Hill, which is 1,729 feet (527 meters) above mean sea level and is Budapest's highest point, tourists may ride an old cog railway, a bus, or a chairlift to the top of the hill. From the town in the valley below, the hills of Buda, with their attractive forested roads, are easily accessible by any of the aforementioned forms of transportation. To travel to the top of Buda's hills from the town below, you may take a chairlift, an old-fashioned cog train, or a bus. Any of these options will make the trip fast and easy. The Children's Railway, sometimes referred to as the Gyermekvast, is a train that runs through the hills and is mostly managed by children. This train is also known as the Gyermekvast.

Both the Pest megye and the Buda járás have their administrative headquarters in Budapest, which is also the location of the Hungarian government's administrative headquarters. There are a total of 23 administrative districts in the city, six of which are located on the Buda side, sixteen of which are located in Pest, and one of which is located on Csepel Island. Although Budapest has a chief mayor in addition to the mayors of its administrative districts, each district also has its government and its mayor. Officially, the city is managed by the General Assembly of Budapest, which is consisting of 34 individuals. This assembly includes the mayor of Budapest, the mayors of the city's 23 districts, and 9 members selected from "compensation party lists."

The city has a long tradition of providing superior public services, at least in the heart of the business district (gas was made available there for private users in the year 1856, and electricity was first implemented there in the year 1893) as evidenced by the renovations made to the telephone system and the public transportation system in the 1970s. In addition, gas was made available there for private users in the year 1856, and electricity was introduced there in the year 1893. It is not necessary to have any more social services or hospital care, particularly in the core commercial center of the city. Despite this, the suicide rate in the city of Budapest is at an alarmingly high level.

Cultural life

The prominent position that Budapest has in Hungarian culture is a substantial contributor to the already thriving economy of the city of Budapest. It is generally accepted that the publishing business, the media industry (which includes radio and television broadcasting), and the film industry are the exclusive preserve of the nation's capital. Despite this stereotype, Budapest has been a magnet for writers, poets, and other artists who are overly preoccupied with country living and the people who live there. At one time or another in their careers, composers like Ferenc Erkel, Ernst von Dohnányi, Béla Bartók, and Zoltán Kodály all made the nation's capital city home. The Hungarian National Gallery may also be found in the city of Budapest. As a result of the city of Budapest being home to a number of the country's most prestigious primary schools, the vast majority of the most academically gifted children in the nation choose to continue their education at one of the city's universities or colleges. In addition, the Hungarian Academy of Sciences and the great majority of Hungary's research institutes may be located in Budapest. This city is the scientific hub of Hungary.

Attend a show at the Vgsznház, which is generally recognized as being among the most prestigious theaters in the whole of Hungary.

Attend a show at the Vgsznház, which is generally recognized as being among the most prestigious theaters in the whole of Hungary. View any videos that are relevant to this topic by clicking here.

In addition, Budapest is home to some of the best orchestras, sports facilities, and theaters in all of Hungary, as well as some of the country's greatest libraries, museums, and art galleries. It was in the year 1802 that the Hungarian National Museum was formed, and it now houses an extensive collection of historical and archaeological items. Franz Liszt, a pianist, and composer, established the music institution in 1875, and in the years since then, it has garnered a considerable amount of notoriety all over the globe. In 1984, the beauty that the Opera House had when it was first built in the 19th century was brought back to life. The National Theatre complex has a sizable park as well as a sculpture garden inside its boundaries. It was completed in 2002, and its current location is on the Pest side of the Rákóczi Bridge, which is located across the Danube. The Mupa Budapest, also known as the Palace of Fine Art, Budapest, has been open to the public since 2005 and can be found just next door. The Béla Bartók National Concert Hall, the Festival Theatre, the Ludwig Museum (which shows contemporary art), and a few more venues may all be found at this site. Collectively, they provide platforms for performances of a wide range of styles of dance, opera, jazz, dance, and other forms of the performing arts. These forms include popular music as well as classical music.

Located in the capital city of Islamabad, the Pakistan Monument is a famous monument that has sculptural depictions of each of Pakistan's four provinces.

A Test on Country Names and Capital Cities, Provided by Britannica Quiz

There are more than the city's fair share of bookshops in Budapest, an astonishing number of hairdressing salons and swimming pools (occasionally the two may be combined), and a vast choice of thermal spas to choose from. In addition, there is a diverse selection of thermal spas in Budapest. Radium and maybe other minerals can be discovered in the many underground hot springs that are located below the surface of the earth. Since Roman times, people have thought that these hot springs had healing properties, which has led to their popularity among bathers.

HISTORY OF BUDAPEST

There is considerable evidence of human settlement on the western bank of the Danube going back to the Neolithic period and farther in antiquity. The nature of the land makes Budapest's location an excellent site for human habitation, and this evidence can be found dating back to the Neolithic period. In the region that was destined to become Buda, the Celtic Eravisci established a hamlet that they named Ak-Ink (which means "Ample Water") around two kilometers to the north of Castle Hill. The Romans established a military camp and a civilian colony at the site that would eventually become known as Aquincum at the end of the first century CE. The Romans called the place Aquincum. Aquincum grew into a lively urban center with two amphitheaters when it became the capital of the province Pannonia Inferior (about the year 106) when it attained the title of a municipium (around the year 124), and finally when it became a full colony (194). Both of the amphitheaters were built during Aquincum's time as the capital of Pannonia Inferior. After the collapse of Roman rule in Pannonia in the early 5th century, some of the large structures in the region were taken by the Huns, and then later on, by the Visigoths and the Avars; each group held control of the land for a period during which they inhabited the buildings. The Huns were followed by the Visigoths and the Avars.

It is believed that at the end of the ninth century, the Magyar tribal chieftain known as Kurszán moved his family into the palace that had previously been held by the Roman ruler. After Stephen I of Hungary established a Christian kingdom in the early 11th century, the settlement migrated farther south to Castle Hill at some point during or soon after that period. Castle Hill was either the location of the settlement at the time, or it took place during that time. It is believed that the first constable of the new fortification that was built on Castle Hill was a man named Buda. The town was named after him. "Old Buda" was the name given to the old site, which was to the north of the new fortification and is today known as "Buda." On the other bank of the river was the Slavonic settlement of Pest, which had been there for some time. The name Pest comes from the Hungarian word for "lime kiln," which is also the meaning of the German name for Buda, Ofen.

During the whole of the medieval ages, the Hungarian royal court served as Buda's sponsor, and the rise and fall of the city correlated with the fortunes of the court. The town was formally established in 1244 when King Béla IV issued a royal charter, which is considered to be the origin of the town. He gave the people of Pest, whose town had been destroyed by the Mongols in 1241, permission to live in the walled castle while still retaining all of their rights. This was a very kind act on his part. He did this as a gesture of respect for the Mongols, who had been responsible for the destruction of the Pest. Before its restructuring in 1439, the municipal government had been managed by Germans. During this time, it had remained compliant with

German law and been under the jurisdiction of German burghers. During that period, parity status was awarded to Hungarians who were working in roles that were part of the local government. Buda's preeminence, which developed under royal protection, was emphasized by its judicial jurisdiction (as a higher court) over other free royal towns. Although the proximity of the king's court hindered the city's potential for self-government, Buda's preeminence was highlighted by its judicial jurisdiction (as a higher court). Even though Matthias, I was the one responsible for the renovation of the palace, his death in 1490 marked the beginning of the decline of royal power as well as the town. The Turks were able to keep their authority over Buda from the years 1541 to 1686. It was finally liberated by a Christian army headed by Leopold I, who was the Emperor of the Holy Roman Empire at the time. This occurred after a lengthy and intense siege. By the 18th century, just a minuscule piece of Matthias's Buda was still standing.

Buda, Óbuda, and Pest

In the year 1703, King Leopold I of Belgium announced that both Buda and Pest would henceforth be independent royal cities. At that time, Buda was little more than a small hamlet that was located inside Pest Megye. Pest Megye was an autonomous county that was governed by the Hungarian aristocrats who lived in the area. In the year 1720, the population of Pest was just 2,600, while the combined population of Buda and Buda was around 9,600. However, by the year 1799, the population of Buda had decreased to around 24,300, while the population of Pest had increased to 29,870, demonstrating that the ratio of the size of the two townships had shifted.

Pest, a German commercial city in Hungary that was already a part of the Habsburg Empire of Austria, began to witness a major population increase in the latter half of the 18th century. This was when the Habsburgs ruled Austria. Even though German Roman Catholics were the only people who were allowed to stay in Buda at the beginning of the 18th century, Buda continued to function as an imperial garrison town and flourished once again under the careful eye of the emperor. This was even though at the beginning of the 18th century, the only people who were authorized to reside there were Germans. A brand-new royal home was built in the 1760s under the reign of Maria Theresa

(1740–1778). This construction took place in Vienna. The university had been situated in Nagyszombat, which is now the city of Trnava in Slovakia. In 1777, it was moved to its current site in Buda, which is also in Hungary. In 1949, the university received its current name, Loránd Eotvos University. In the year 1783, Joseph II moved the administrative headquarters of the kingdom to Buda. In the same year, the location of the Curia, which is also referred to as the High Court, was changed to Buda. Pest, on the other hand, was chosen to serve as the site of the educational institution. Floods were a problem for many centuries, and one that occurred in 1838 took an exceptionally terrible toll: more than half of the dwellings in Pest were destroyed, and Buda also suffered from the consequences of the flood. In 1838, floods took an especially catastrophic toll.

STUNNING ATTRACTIONS IN BUDAPEST

It is widely accepted that Budapest is one of the most beautiful cities in all of Europe; hence, it should not come as a surprise that Budapest has for a very long time been a popular site for holidaymakers. Throughout its long and illustrious history, Budapest, the largest city in Hungary and also the capital of the country, has been ruled by several distinct groups of people, including the Romans, the Ottomans, and the Austro-Hungarians, amongst others. Today, Budapest serves as the nation's capital. As a direct consequence of this, the city is crammed to the gills with fascinating historical landmarks, eye-popping museums, and unique forms of architectural design.

The city of Budapest, which is located on both banks of the Danube River, is sometimes referred to as the "City of Spas" because of the abundance of hot springs that are situated above the city. In the past, Budapest was composed of two distinct towns: Buda, which was situated on the western side of the river, and Pest, which was situated on the eastern bank of the river. It wasn't until the year 1873 that the two cities merged into one.

In addition to the city's numerous other sites of interest and attractions, the wrecked bars in the Jewish Quarter serve as the hub of Budapest's active nightlife scene. This is another reason why the city is so well-known as a tourist destination. Since Budapest is undeniably one of the most fascinating towns in Central Europe, visitors should make it a point to stop there at some point during their vacation.

1. Hungarian Parliament Building

It is utterly mind-boggling to view the sheer scale and enormity of the Hungarian Parliament Building, which is the largest building in the whole country of Hungary. It fully dominates everything in its immediate neighborhood, thus it is impossible not to notice its presence. It is generally agreed upon that the gigantic edifice that is located on the banks of the Danube River is one of the most recognizable landmarks in the city. Its two symmetrical facades are elaborately decorated with sculptures of prominent figures in Hungarian history, and they lie on either side of a massive dome that exudes majesty. The structure is widely regarded as being among the most outstanding examples of Gothic Revival architecture found in the surrounding region.

The inside, which was completed in 1904, is every bit as stunning as the outside, and tours take tourists to explore the Golden Staircase, the Dome Hall, and the Congress Hall. Within the Parliament, there are a total of 691 rooms, and each one outdoes the one that came before it in terms of the exquisiteness of its interior design. When visiting Budapest, one must ensure that they do not miss out on the opportunity to see the Hungarian Parliament Building as it is one of the most popular tourist destinations in the city and is an absolute must-see among the numerous wonders that Budapest has to offer. The structure, which dates back to 1896 even though it is still in use by the national government in the present day, was erected in that year.

2. The hill above Castle

A breathtaking panorama of the city of Budapest, as well as the Danube River, can be seen from the top of Castle Hill, which is situated on the Buda side of the city. Despite its relatively modest size, the hill is home to a number of the most historically important and aesthetically stunning sights that the nation's capital has to offer. Matthias Church, the Fisherman's Bastion, and Buda Tower are among the attractions that may be found atop the hill, in addition to Buda Castle and its impressive collection of museums.

Beautiful examples of Baroque, Gothic, and Neoclassical architecture can be found throughout the Old Town and the complex of the Royal Palace, making it a great delight to take a walk around these places. The Old Town is also home to some of the oldest buildings in the complex. The Old Town is made up of small winding alleyways made of cobblestone, while the Royal Palace complex is home to some very stunning buildings. An excellent method to get to the top of the hill is to take the lovely old Castle Hill Funicular that trundles its way up the mountain. This funicular has been operating at that location for quite some time now.

3. Szechenyi Bath

Even though Budapest is home to a myriad of beautiful thermal baths that you may visit, none of them can compare to the reputation and popularity of Szechenyi, which is the largest spa complex in all of Europe. If you want to experience a spa like no other, you should go to Szechenyi. The expansive facilities, which were built in 1913 and are located in a lovely Neo-Baroque building that is bright yellow, provide visitors the option to make use of saunas, steam rooms, and, of course, thermal pools. The building that houses the amenities is wonderful and brilliant yellow.

Because of the plethora of fine decorations that can be seen here, such as mosaics, sculptures, and chandeliers, it is an excellent location for unwinding and taking some much-needed relaxation. The ambiance is typically tranquil, even though it may get very crowded; that is unless you go there during one of its Saturday night pool parties, in which case the environment is anything from tranquil. Szechenyi Bath in Budapest, often known as the "City of Spas," is a destination that simply must be visited to fully appreciate what it means to be in the "City of Spas."

4. St. Stephen's Basilica

As a result of its magnificent size and the fact that it nearly entirely blocks out the sky, the front of St. Stephen's Basilica offers an amazing vista. The massive Roman Catholic basilica, which was given its current name after Hungary's first king, also has two sturdy bell towers and a large dome on the top of its structure. It is enclosed on all sides by a spacious courtyard. Its expansive interior is brilliantly decorated, and hidden among the sturdy marble columns are several spectacular mosaics, sculptures, and paintings that may be found hidden away within.

Even though it wasn't built until 1905, St. Stephen's is largely regarded as the most important church in the country, and it continues to be a center of activity to this day, holding choral performances, classical concerts, and daily religious services. Even though it wasn't finished until 1905, St. Stephen's is widely regarded as the most significant church in the nation.

5. Buda Castle

The huge Buda Castle and palace complex is a fascinating destination to see and was once the abode of Hungarian emperors and queens in days gone by. The complex also has several palaces. The majestic Baroque castle was built on Castle Hill in 1265, and it sits at one of the ends of the hill. It is the present home of the Hungarian National Gallery as well as the Budapest History Museum, both of which are fantastic attractions that should not be missed and are both located in one building.

The former museum presents an amazing collection of paintings, sculptures, and prints, while the latter exhibits a broad range of intriguing artifacts that take visitors on a journey through Budapest's tumultuous past. Both museums may be found inside the city of Budapest. Since it is just a short distance away from many of the city's most prominent attractions, the Buda Castle is a great location for anybody interested in the city's art, history, and architecture.

6. Szechenyi Chain Bridge

When it was shown to the general public for the first time in the year 1849, the Szechenyi Chain Bridge was lauded as both a technical wonder and a symbol of Hungary's reemergence and reawakening for the country. The bridge, which was constructed out of cast iron, was the nation's first-ever permanent crossing over the Danube.

It established a connection between the two cities of Buda and Pest and had a role in bringing the East and the West into a location that was physically closer to one another.

In addition to the magnificent architecture that is on show, the bridge also has some remarkable decorative elements. These components include four statues of lions that stand out due to their unique appearance, one of which is located at each end of the bridge. Because of the breathtaking effect that the Szechenyi Chain Bridge's lighting has at night, it is one of the locations in the city that is often the subject of photographs.

7. Margaret Island

Since it is situated in the middle of the Danube and is mostly comprised of magnificently green parks, Margaret Island is a very pleasant and picturesque area in which to spend some time as a result of its advantageous position. The island is connected to the northern and southern parts of Budapest employing the Arpad Bridge and the Margaret Bridge, respectively. In addition, the island has a water park, an athletics facility, and a myriad of attractive paths and trails.

As a consequence of this, it has become a very well-liked area for recreation not just among locals but also among tourists. In addition to being home to some fascinating ruins from the medieval ages, it also has an entertaining Music Fountain.

8. The Fisherman's Bastion

The enchanting Fisherman's Bastion, which can be located within Buda Castle, is often recognized as one of the top spots to see in Budapest, and this reputation is well earned. The Fisherman's Bastion can be found inside Buda

Castle. Its dazzlingly bright white walls are broken up by seven elegant and intricate towers, each of which is named after one of the seven Hungarian chieftains who were responsible for creating the country in the year 895. The stronghold occupies a precarious foothold on the ridge of the summit.

It wasn't until 1902 that construction began on the bastion, and it was given its name in honor of the fishermen's guild that had been charged in the past with the responsibility of guarding this portion of the city's defenses. In addition to marveling at the magnificent Neo-Romanesque architecture of the structure, visitors can also take in a breathtaking view of the Danube and the Hungarian Parliament Building. The time of day right before sunset is an especially lovely time to pay a visit to the building, since this is when the view is at its most breathtaking.

9. The Cathedral of Saint Matthew

Because of its stunning position exactly next to the Fishermen's Bastion, the Matthias Church is often considered to be one of the most appealing buildings in the whole city, and with good reason: it is situated in the heart of the city. When the sun shines on the building's light-colored bricks, it gives off the appearance that the edifice is glittering right in front of your eyes. Its gorgeous facade and tall spire are both superb specimens of Gothic architecture. Because the previous church was razed to the ground by the Mongols in the early part of the 14th century, this particular church has a long and eventful history. The second part of that century saw the structure's reconstruction.

Not only was this structure used as a mosque during the time of the Ottomans, but it also served as the site of Franz Joseph I's coronation as Emperor of the Holy Roman Empire. The inside of this edifice is lavishly decorated, which is a fitting choice given the nature of the

Budapest Travel Guide

occasion being held here. Because the Matthias Church in Budapest seems to be just as magical when it is lit up at night as it is during the day, it is an attraction that should not be missed by anybody who is going to that city.

10. Footwear sold along the Danube Riverbank

During World War II, a fascist organization known as the Arrow Cross group briefly held power in Hungary. During this period, they were responsible for the brutal death of 3,500 Jewish people and political opponents. The harrowing story of these victims is memorialized by this monument, which was just constructed in 2005.

The unfortunate victims were rounded up by the militiamen, instructed to take off their shoes, and then shot before their bodies were carried away by the river. The water eventually swept away the victims' bodies. The shoes of the dead were taken by the militiamen after the corpses of the victims had been swept away. The Hungarian Parliament Building is just a short distance away from the moving tributes that take the shape of bronze shoes scattered along the Danube. These shoes are meant to act as a constant reminder of the horrible deaths that occurred to the victims.

11. Citadella

Views of Budapest and the Danube River below may be enjoyed from the Citadella, which is perched on top of Gellert Hill. In the year 1851, the Hapsburgs began building on the fort, and it wasn't until a significant amount of time had passed before the Nazis and, after them, the Communists acquired possession of it. Throughout its existence, the local population has served as both the target of its protection and the instrument of its punishment.

Today, a magnificent Liberation Monument can be seen perched over it in its current location. Visitors shouldn't skip out on seeing it. Despite the recent decision to make the inside of the fort inaccessible to the general public, the fort's vantage position still provides a magnificent view over the surrounding area, which is sure to steal your breath away.

12. Vajdahunyad Castle

The imaginative design of Vajdahunyad Castle exhibits a dazzling diversity of Baroque, Gothic, Renaissance, and Romanesque features, giving the castle a look that is fairly comparable to that of a setting from a fairytale. This gives the castle the name "Vajdahunyad," which translates to "Vajda's Castle." It was created out of cardboard and wood for the Millennium World Exhibition, and its design was based on a stronghold that may perhaps be located in Transylvania.

Its fantastical qualities, on the other hand, turned out to be so well appreciated by the community that the architect Ignac Alpar's plan was ultimately put into action in the year 1896 by making use of the necessary materials. The weird and fascinating castle can be viewed in City Park, and taking pictures of it offers some incredible options for artistic expression. Both Heroes' Square and Szechenyi Bath, which are situated near one another, may be reached on foot in a very short amount of time.

13. The Great Synagogue

The Great Synagogue, which is also known as the Dohany Street Synagogue, is generally regarded as being among the most important and magnificent buildings in the city. Its original name was the Dohany Street Synagogue. It was built in 1859, and it has some particularly impressive instances of Moorish Revival architecture. The inside, which has exquisite furnishings, is just as beautiful to look at as the front of the building.

It is significant because it is the second-largest synagogue in the world, after the Belz Great Synagogue in Jerusalem; this illustrates just how prominent and big Budapest's Jewish population used to be. It is strongly suggested that you go to the Great Synagogue if you are interested in knowing more about the Jewish history of the city. You may learn a lot by going there. Not only is it connected to the enormous Jewish cemetery that is situated behind it, but it is also connected to a Jewish museum as well as different memorials that memorialize the Holocaust. The Jewish cemetery is located just behind it.

14. Heroes' Square

The massive monument that can be seen in the exact center of Heroes Square serves as the focal point of the area. You may find the plaza at one end of Andrassy Avenue, quite near to where City Park is located. The plaza is dominated by a gigantic column, which is flanked on each side by two elegant colonnades. This piece of writing seems to be aiming for the stars. Statues of well-known and historically important Hungarian national leaders are displayed in each of these with great pride.

At the foot of the column are several sculptures that seem to be even more majestic and epic. These sculptures portray the "Seven Chieftains of the Magyars," who were the first leaders of the country of Hungary. They are known as the "Seven Chieftains of the Magyars." Heroes Plaza is the largest and most prominent plaza in Budapest, and it is bordered on two sides by the Museum of Fine Arts as well as the Palace of Art. Both of these buildings are considered to be cultural landmarks in Hungary.

PARKS AND RESERVES IN BUDAPEST

1. Buda Arboretum

One of the most popular tourist destinations in Budapest is the Buda Arboretum, which is situated in the southern region of the city close to the foot of Gellért Hill. The land that is presently occupied by a nature reserve and the campus of a university was formerly planted with vines that date back to the 19th century. There was an outbreak of phylloxera towards the end of the 19th century, which caused grapes to become extinct. Phylloxera are very few insects that feed on the roots of grapes. However, because of their demise, we are now able to nurture many of the trees, flowers, and shrubs that we hold in high regard. There is a tiny pond and a tropical greenhouse located on Villányi Street, which makes it an excellent starting place for an exploration of the neighborhood that is all around it. During the springtime, flowers are abundant, such as tulips, daffodils, and other varieties of flowers. In addition, if you are coming from Menesit, you have the option of going by a forest that is less visited; nevertheless, the gate is often shut. If you choose this route, however, you should be aware that it may take longer.

2. Budapest Zoo & Botanical Gardens

You may be enticed to go to the zoo only to view the lions and elephants, but the Botanical Garden that is situated on the grounds of the zoo is not something that should be disregarded. In addition to the well-known Palm House, which is home to a variety of tropical flora including banana trees, sago palm trees, and many more, the grounds are home to over 2,000 unique plant species. The grounds also have their Japanese garden. Near this, we come across the citrus garden, which is home to a variety of plant species native to both the Mediterranean and subtropical regions.

3. Budatétényi Rose Garden

This stunning rose garden is spread over an area of 2.5 hectares and has an extensive collection of roses from countries all over the globe. Its location on the hills of Nagytétény is particularly advantageous. The public is invited to visit the garden at any time of the year, and it even serves as a gene bank due to the enormous collection of various sorts of organisms that it houses. During the academic year 1964–1965, the garden was designed following the recommendations made by the Horticultural Research Institute. This collection is considered to be the largest of its kind in Hungary because it is believed to include between 7,000 and 8,000 different varieties of roses. As a consequence of the improvements, tourists will now have the chance to sit down and seek shelter from the rain while admiring the natural beauty of the park. This is one of the many benefits that the visitors will get as a direct result of the restorations.

4. ELTE Botanical Gardens

This stunning work of horticultural art can be discovered tucked away in District VIII, and it is an attraction that should not be missed under any circumstances. Its history can be traced back to the 1700s, and it has more than 12,000 plant species that are different from one another. During the warmer months, guests are welcome to wander the large grounds at no cost; however, the many greenhouses guarantee that guests may satiate their need for plants at any time of the year. Even the ageless classic "The Boys on Pál Street" authored by Ferenc Molnár includes a casual allusion to the gardens. Those who have a passion for plants are going to find the botanical shop that is located on the premises to be of great interest. The store sells plants that were cultivated from the various specimens that can be found within the park. These plants can often not be found anywhere else in the city, thus this is a unique opportunity to purchase them.

5. Japanese Garden located on Margaret Island

A great number of travelers visit this well-known location on Margaret Island to see the sunbathing turtles and the leisurely, fascinating motions of the beautiful orange koi fish. While they are there, they may also enjoy some of the other attractions that the island has to offer. Although this is not a Japanese garden in the conventional sense – in contrast to Zugló, which was mentioned before – many of the same components can be observed here. Zugló is a Japanese garden in the traditional sense. Since the waters of this region were known to have medicinal benefits as early as the year 1870, the waterfall was built according to the plans of the well-known architect Miklós Ybl. This was done so since the waterfall was located in the same position. The first rock garden was built in 1922, and during the 1930s, a Japanese garden was established all around the rock garden. The rock garden was the centerpiece of the Japanese garden. The garden has later been upgraded with the installation of new plant species, as well as seating spaces that have been created in the manner of conventional Japanese architecture.

6. Japanese Garden in Szentendre

This breathtaking garden is conveniently accessible from Budapest by HÉV train, ferry, or bus and can be reached in a short amount of time. It is the perfect spot to go to get away from the rush and bustle of the city for the weekend and spend some time relaxing. It is possible to visit this beautiful Japanese garden in Szentendre, which is located right adjacent to Czóbel Park, free of charge. Since it first opened its doors four years ago, the garden has been designed in such a way that it accommodates each of the four distinct seasons. Evergreens and forest pines make up the evergreen component of the forest, which is representative of the winter season. On the other hand, sakura, also known as Japanese cherry trees, predominates throughout the springtime. In the summer, the lake is filled with water lilies, lotus blooms, irises, and Japanese anemones, while in the fall, maple trees line the edges of the area. The fall season and the summer season share the same area.

7. Mór Jókai Rose Garden

The novelist Mor Jókai used the proceeds from the sale of his first book to acquire a piece of property in 1853 that was deserted, wild, and rocky and was situated on the location of an old quarry. The park is the product of a great deal of hard work, innovative thinking, and extensive study into a wide variety of plant species over many years. The rose garden was a source of particular pride; it continues to exist to this day and is the permanent home of a large number of rare and unusual species of roses. Even though the author's house was demolished due to the lack of upkeep it received, the grounds are still accessible to the general public, and visitors may see a large number of different bird species there. Since 1975, the Jókai Garden has functioned as a conservation area for the flora and wildlife of the surrounding region.

BUDAPEST'S BEST MUSEUMS

The city of Budapest is always teeming with life and bustle. The nightlife is on par with that of any city in Europe, and the city's restaurant scene is fast increasing, which is attracting guests who are enthusiastic about food from all over the globe. Pay a visit to the best museums the city has to offer to get a deeper comprehension of the interesting history and unique customs of this magnificent destination.

1. Hungarian National Museum

Because it seems to be an enormous ancient Greek temple from the era in question, you won't have any trouble finding this museum on Mzeum Kort (which is a section of the Small Boulevard). When revolutionaries who were hostile to the Habsburg monarchy gathered on the steps of the Hungarian National Museum in the year 1848, the museum acted as the hub of the rebellion. It is now the largest museum in the country and has an extensive collection of archaeological findings and artifacts that date back to the period when the communist dictatorship was in power. In contrast to the Budapest History Museum, the scope of this museum encompasses not only the history of the nation of Hungary but also the history of the Carpathian Basin as a whole.

2. The Exhibition Hall of the National Museum of Hungary

The enormous collection, which is held within the royal seat of Buda Castle, traces the creative history of the country, beginning with medieval triptychs and continuing up to art and sculpture made after 1945. The collection is housed inside Buda Castle. The inside of the royal dome, which has magnificent sculptures that resemble wires, is one of the most impressive aspects of the structure. During the high season for tourists, it is possible to scale the structure to the top, where there is an observation deck, provided that the weather is good. Be sure to check out the realist masterpieces made by Mihály Munkácsy as well as the surreal landscapes painted by Tivadar Csontváry Kosztka when you get the chance.

3. The Museum of Fine Arts

The doors of the Museum of Fine Arts, which overlooks Heroes' Square and had been shut for a few years owing to repairs, were eventually unlocked and opened to a great deal of enthusiasm on the day that they were shown to the public. The Romanesque main hall, which had been closed to the public ever since a bomb devastated it during the Second World War, has only just reopened with a colorful cast of characters frescoed onto its gold-fringed walls. The explosion that destroyed the hall occurred during the war. This incredible collection of great art is housed on five floors, and it comprises pieces of art from as far back as ancient Egypt, Greece, and Rome and continuing up to Baroque art. The show features works by artists such as El Greco, Titian, and Raphael. One of the centerpieces of the exhibit is a horse sculpture that is said to have been produced by Leonardo da Vinci.

4. Agricultural Museum

Visits to this restaurant are worth the effort just because of its location in the heart of City Park. The majestic Vajdahunyad Castle, which was constructed in the 19th century and was fashioned after a castle in Transylvania, is home to the Vajdahunyad Museum of Agriculture, which is an equally spectacular structure. Frescoes and chandeliers may be seen adorning the inside of the museum's many halls and rooms. The collection is a hodgepodge of various items, including old farm equipment, taxidermied animals, and a mountain of antlers, among other things.

5. Zwack Unicum Museum

Unicum is a digestive liquor that has a flavor that is best described as being on the bitter side, and it can be found at any restaurant or bar in Hungary. Tours of the factory at its original site in the IX District might provide light on the closely guarded family recipe, which is composed of more than 40 different kinds of herbs and spices. You will have free reign over the cellars and even try a shot straight from the barrel if you so want. In addition, there is a display of the world's largest collection of miniature bottles, which has absolutely nothing to do with the other activities that are being offered.

6. The Hungarian National Museum in Budapest

In the book-filled museum that is housed in the southern wing of Buda Castle, guests have the opportunity to gain knowledge about the history of Budapest, starting with ancient periods and continuing up to the era of communist rule. Even though the most interesting things in the collection are in the basement, it still has things like Roman relics, ruins from the Ottoman Empire, medieval tapestries, and Gothic sculptures. All of these things are fascinating in their own right. This section of Buda Castle is home to the castle's oldest apartments, as well as vaulted vaults and a tall chapel that goes back to the 14th century.

7. Holocaust Memorial Museum

A synagogue that was constructed in the 1920s and later converted into a moving and modern exhibition space can be found in the IX District. Visit this museum to learn about the history of the Holocaust in Hungary, and it will transport you back in time. You may encounter some horrific depictions of the concentration camps as you go along the route. The museum is not simple to see. The exhibition features personal objects such as pens, eyeglasses, and toys, in addition to interactive and static displays, installations, and other types of exhibitions. When you reach the end of the chambers that are scarcely lighted, you will find that you have emerged into the open and spacious blue hall of the historic synagogue.

8. Hungary's National Museum of Photography and Film

When you take a trip along Nagymez Utca, which is situated just off Andrássy Avenue, you have a good chance of coming across a lovely residence that is decorated with ceramics and paintings. This home was once owned by the photographer Mai Manó, who was active in the 19th century and served as a photographer for both the imperial and royal courts. The structure now serves as the home of a museum that is focused on photography from Hungary. In addition to Manó's refurbished former studio, which serves as the primary attraction of the venue, this peculiar museum has a lot of other wonderful exhibitions as well.

9. Budapest Pinball Museum

Budapest Travel Guide

Looking for something that has a little bit more of a comedic edge to it? Then, if you are in the Jlipót area, make your way down to this unusual basement, where you will find Europe's largest interactive museum dedicated to pinball machines. The museum is housed in a building that dates back to the 1920s. When you enter the establishment, there are around 130 retro gaming systems that are turned on and ready to be played. (there is no need to carry any change with you; once you have your ticket, you are free to play on as many as you would like). You may want to have a look at a Humpty Dumpty game from the 1940s. It was one of the very first video games that use flipper bumpers. Certain games date back to the 1880s; however, these are not pinball machines but rather bagatelles, which were the forerunners of pinball machines. certain of the games date back to that period.

10. Ludwig Museum

A multi-building arts complex known as the Millennium Quarter can be found in a section of Pest that was once an industrial district. The Millennium Quarter would be incomplete without the presence of the Ludwig Museum. It shares the same cutting-edge architecture as the Palace of Arts, a music hall that is famous for its cutting-edge technology, with which it shares its location. This contemporary art museum boasts an impressive pop art collection, which includes the works of modern painters such as Andy Warhol, Roy Lichtenstein, and other contemporary artists, in addition to modern art from nations in Central and Eastern Europe.

CHAPTER 2

BEST BEACHES IN BUDAPEST

Even though there aren't too many visitors in Hungary, the beaches there are often packed with individuals from Budapest who are looking to escape the oppressive heat of the city. As a result of this, the atmosphere at these beaches is often laid-back, and you'll have the chance to enjoy the summer in the same manner as Hungarians do.

After you have finished seeing the most important sights in the city and you are ready to relax and get some much-needed air conditioning during the hot summer months, pack your beach towel and swimsuit and go out to one of these beaches in the Budapest area.

1. Go to the Római Part of Budapest and swim in the Danube.

If you are wondering whether or not it is possible to go swimming in the Danube in Budapest, the answer is yes; however, there are special laws that must be observed. If you are wondering whether or not it is possible to go swimming in the Danube in Budapest, the answer is yes. It is now possible to go swimming in the Danube on the section of beach that has been dedicated for this purpose at Római-Parti Plázs till the late hour of 10 p.m. during July and August. Because of the poor quality of the water, swimming in the river was made illegal in the 1970s. The good news is that the river's water is now safe to swim in, and the ban on bathing in the Danube has been abolished as of the year 2023.

Római Part sometimes referred to as Roman Beach is a beach that can be found in the Buda district of Budapest, which lies on the northern side of the city and directly across the Danube River. Its tree-lined pebbled beach is a popular destination for visitors from all over the city due to the grungy riverfront bars that are housed in converted double-decker buses and the vintage seafood sellers that can be found there. If you'd rather just relax by the river with a focus (spritzer) in your hand, go on over to the Fellini Római Kultrbisztró, where you can pick up a colorful deckchair that's right on the water's edge. Those who are content with doing little more than that will find the place to be ideal. Because there is a bike path that parallels the Danube from the city center all the way out to Római Part, coming here on two wheels is not at all difficult.

2. Siófok Beach

Lake Balaton, often known as the "Hungarian Sea," is only a little over an hour away by rail, so if you want to spend the day in the "Hungarian Sea," all you have to do is get on a train and go in that direction. The town of Siofok is the largest resort on Lake Balaton, and its main beach is famous for being not only one of the most popular waterside hangouts in the country but also a major party destination during the warm summer months. This beach is located in the town of Siofok, which is located in Hungary.

The day tickets to access the grassy beach that is filled with cafés, restaurants, loungers, and even a giant Ferris wheel are relatively reasonable to purchase. This beach is also located close to Petfi Promenade, which is a promenade that is well-known during the summer months for its vibrant nightlife and busy clubs. If you want to bring the party right down to the beach, you should go to Plázs in the evening. There, you'll find concerts, foam parties, and other paid activities going place.

3. Kopaszi Gát and BudaPart

The Lágymányosi Bay is partly isolated from the Danube by the refurbished region of Kopaszi gát (Kopaszi dam) and Budapest (Buda Beach), which is situated in the up-and-coming District XI on the southern side of the city. Kopaszi gát literally translates to "Kopaszi dam." It is filled to the brim with lush parks, trendy pubs such as Durer Kert (which has moved from City Park), restaurants that provide street food and gastropub cuisine with a view of the beach, and plenty of sandy stretches where one may put a towel down. Despite this, swimming is not permitted on any of these beaches, even though they are free for anybody to use. The only spot in the vicinity of the dam where swimming is permitted and considered to be safe is inside the area marked off by buoys on Sho Beach. Sho Beach is a section of the coast that requires admission fees and is furnished with bars, loungers, changing facilities, showers, and food sellers that line the boardwalk. At this site, you may rent stand-up paddleboards to get your paddleboarding fix.

The heavy rainfall that might occur in Budapest during the summer months adds to the increasing volumes of water that can be found in the Danube. This suggests that the beaches that are located along the Danube may get inundated, which will lead them to "disappear" beneath the water.

3. Nagymaros Beach

A little town known as Nagymaros may be found tucked between the Borzsony Hills and the Danube River in the most attractive area of the Danube Bend. The Danube River flows through the middle of the town. The free, sandy beach that overlooks the hills is a magnificent place that is popular with inhabitants in the area as well as a population that is believed to be more bohemian. This gorgeous location is popular with residents in the vicinity since it is a gorgeous setting.

On the other bank from the town are a group of hills known together as the Pilis Hills. These hills are covered in a thick forest. Because it is placed so precariously high above the river, the Visegrad Citadel makes this beach an exceptional spot for photographing photographs. If you find yourself in need of something to eat or drink, there are a few kiosks that provide fish in addition to lángos, which is a pastry that is deep-fried and coated with sour cream and cheese. If you find yourself in need of something to eat or drink, you may visit one of these kiosks. You may also sit down under the vine-covered courtyard at Piknik Manufaktura, which attracts a varied crowd that spans from alternative types to digital nomads who work in the OOO Campus, a coworking space that is located on the terrace above the bar. Piknik Manufaktura is a place where you can find a variety of people. Approximately half an hour of following the river to the north will get you to Nomad Bar. It is known for having a vibe that is reminiscent of a hippie commune. At this hub for countercultural creation, you will have the opportunity to take a break by the river, where you may unwind in a hammock with a drink in your hand or go for a paddle with a few other people who share your values.

5. Lupa Beach

The ambiance at Lupa Beach is the one that is most comparable to that of a beach resort with five stars that you'll discover anyplace in the vicinity of Budapest. This historic mining lake is home to some of the cleanest water you'll find anywhere in Hungary, and it's framed on all sides by pristine beaches, towering palm trees, and plush loungers with four posts apiece.

You won't even miss the ocean if you go for a swim in the water that is gin-pure, go for a swim in the water that is crystal clear, and sink your toes into the sand since you can grab a beverage or enjoy fine eating on the beach (the restaurant Costes, which has a Michelin star, has a catering stand here). It is possible to reach Lupa Lake and its beach by a direct bus trip of thirty minutes that departs directly from the Nyugati train station, which is located in the center of Budapest.

6. Lake Velence beaches

Lake Velence, which is Hungary's third-largest natural lake and can be reached from Budapest in approximately half an hour by train, is also the country's most accessible lake. It is one of the warmest in Europe, with temperatures ranging between 82 and 78 degrees Fahrenheit, and it is rich in minerals such as salt and magnesium. It is also one of the most mineral-rich.

The Velence Korzó is a public beach that can be found on Lake Velence. The Velence train station may be reached on foot in only a few minutes from the beach at Velence Korzó. In the summer, it is often packed with locals who come here for the seaside atmosphere, which includes lángos and street-food kiosks, restaurants, and cafés, as well as, among other things, facilities for sports and watersports. There are stretches of sandy beach that run along to the water's edge, and guests may rent sun loungers and sunshades along with other beach amenities such as safety deposit boxes, changing rooms, and bathrooms. It is possible to find free beaches that are less crowded at Gárdony, which is situated along the lake one rail stop after the railway station in Velence. Gárdony may be reached by taking the train. Hidden from public view is one of these beaches, which caters only to nudists.

BEST PLACES TO STAY IN BUDAPEST

Although the city of Budapest as a whole is home to around 1.9 million people, the central districts of the city are packed into a relatively small space. This suggests that even if you want to stay in an area that is close to a particular destination or activity, it is not difficult to walk to other regions or use public transit to go there. This is the case even if you choose to stay in a location that is close to a particular destination or activity. There is not a single neighborhood that is universally acknowledged as being the best for tourists; the Castle District, Parliament, and Belváros are the areas that are home to the majority of the city's most important historical sites, yet the Jewish Quarter is renowned for its nightlife culture that is just incredible. There are some hotels located in the Castle District, which is a more romantic choice since it sets you amid cobblestone pathways and buildings reminiscent of a fairy tale. In and around Belváros and the Jewish Quarter is where you'll find the greatest number of hotels close to one another. Even if some districts are farther from the regions that are visited by visitors, the possibilities that can be found in such communities might still be attractive.

1. On the western bank of the Danube, you'll find the neighborhood that's often referred to as the Castle District (District I). Both the Matthias Church and the Royal Palace, two of the most stunning sights in the city, may be found in this mountainous area of the city. During the busiest parts of the day (the daytime), which include the summer months, holidays, and weekends, the best time to visit this area is either early in the morning or late in the evening. If you want to avoid crowds, the best time to visit is either early in the morning or late in the evening. The great majority of Budapest's thermal baths may be found inside and slightly outside of this territory, including the Rudas Baths, which can be found immediately to the south of Elizabeth Bridge. These baths are considered to be something of an anomaly since they are situated within this zone. Even though this is a somewhat touristy location, there are still quite a few fantastic restaurants to be found here, and the southern portions offer a lot of cool nightlife establishments to choose from. On the Pest side of the river, one may go everywhere they need to go on foot or by using the public transit system.

2. The areas along the river's west bank and in the river itself that are known as Buda, Margaret Island, and Buda Hills (District III) are recognized for the relative peace that can be found there. (this is especially true about Margaret Island). Buda has the ambiance of a quaint small town, complete with attractive old buildings and a wide selection of restaurants serving delectable cuisine. The Roman ruins at Aquincum are the key attraction in this region; as a result of the large amounts of open space and educational possibilities that are available there, it is a perfect vacation for families. In the Buda Hills, which are situated in Budapest, common recreational pursuits include walking, mountain biking, and, during the winter months, sledding. Another activity that young children find to be quite fun is the Children's Train, which is run here by the children themselves under the supervision of adults. On Margaret Island, one may find a variety of parks, and a swimming pool, in addition to a huge number of open places. No matter where in the city you go, there is a good chance that you will be treated to stunning views of the Pest bank of the Danube River.

3. The neighborhood surrounding the Parliament (District V) is remarkably quiet, considering its closeness to some of the noisiest sections of downtown Budapest. Its elegant streets are placed relatively close to the river, and there are lots of sights as well as many wonderful restaurants in the region, which makes it a perfect place to stay if you don't want to be right in the thick of the action, but you still want to be close to it. The stunning building that serves as the location of the Hungarian Parliament never fails to wow guests, no matter how many times they step foot inside. At Liberty Square Park, in addition to having lovely vegetation, there is a fountain, which is a favorite spot for children to play in.

4. Belváros (area V), which is close to the south of the area that houses the Parliament, is the district that serves as the beating heart of downtown Budapest. In addition to significant buildings like St. Stephen's Cathedral and Váci Street, which is the most famous shopping district in the city, this area is bustling with vibrant restaurants and cafés. In this area, in addition to inhabitants of all hues and tourists from far and wide, you may find a significant number of major hotels. This district extends to the northeast into Teréváros (District VI), which has a more neighborhood-like vibe (although it is still very busy and urban) and is home to attractions like the House of Terror Museum and the Hungarian Opera House. This region is known as the Pest side.

5. The section of the city with the highest population density is known as the Jewish Quarter (District VII), and it may be found to the

southeast of Belváros. In addition to this, it is jam-packed to the gills with pubs and clubs, the most famous of which are the city's Ruin Pubs. These establishments are located in graffiti-covered, dilapidated buildings that date back to the communist period or earlier. The name of the neighborhood alludes to the fact that there is a significant amount of Jewish culture to be found in this region, and the Great Synagogue, along with a few other, smaller temples and kosher dining establishments, are all contributors to this culture. Additionally, this neighborhood is home to several hip cafes and shops. This is the place to stay in Budapest if you want to experience the city's vibrant nightlife scene from the point of view of a young, trendy, and grungy (in the best possible manner) crowd.

6. If you go south to the Palace District (Jószefváros, District VIII), you'll discover a University vibe with cheaper restaurants, some amazing old libraries, and a decidedly less touristy feel, even though this is still thoroughly close to the sights and restaurants of the city center and is only to a 15- to 20-minute walk to Ruin Pubs and the Jewish Quarter. This is because the Palace District is located in District VIII. In contrast to its noisy and disorganized ambiance, this neighborhood is well-known for the bohemian and intellectual ambiance of its nightlife, including its restaurants and cafés. In addition to this, it is the site of the Hungarian National Museum, which is sometimes cited as being the most impressive attraction in the city.

Even though it is just a quarter of an hour's walk or a fifteen-minute Metro ride from the city center, the City Park neighborhood (District

XIV) is considered to be somewhat farther out from the core of the city. This district is home to several important tourist destinations, including Heroes Square, the San Francisco Zoo, and several museums, one of which is the Museum of Fine Arts. In addition, the area is home to a sizable quantity of really exquisite examples of Art Nouveau and Secessionist architecture.

TOP-RATED HOTELS IN BUDAPEST

1. Gresham Palace, A Four Seasons Hotel

The Four Seasons Gresham Palace is a luxurious hotel that can be found in the heart of Budapest, which is located in Hungary. The hotel is part of the Four Seasons brand. This hotel, which has been awarded five stars, is situated on the bank of the Danube River and offers spectacular views of both the city and the river. The hotel's location on the riverbank also makes it one of the most desirable hotels in the area. Because of the hotel's flawless integration of modern amenities and classic design, guests have the opportunity to take part in an experience that will be ingrained in their memories for a very long time.

The Four Seasons Gresham Palace offers its visitors a comprehensive selection of first-rate services and amenities in a broad variety of categories. During their visit, guests have access to a spa that offers a complete range of services, as well as a fitness center and an indoor pool. In addition, the hotel has a variety of restaurants and pubs that offer cuisine not only from the surrounding area but also from other countries and continents. The hotel also has a business center, meeting rooms, and a concierge service that is accessible at all times of the day and night.

2. The Hotel Corinthia.

The Corinthia Hotel Budapest is a well-respected institution that has been awarded five stars, and it can be located right in the middle of Budapest. This hotel is located in a historic building that was built in the year 1896, so guests who are seeking a sophisticated and wonderful place to stay in the middle of the city should give this business considerable consideration since it is situated in the building.

The hotel has an extensive range of amenities and services, such as several excellent eating choices, a spa and wellness center, an indoor pool, and a fitness facility. Furthermore, the hotel provides many rooms that are suitable for hosting a variety of different types of meetings and events. In addition, visitors have access to a front desk that is manned continuously, free wireless internet, services to hire vehicles, and laundry facilities.

The hotel offers a choice of rooms and suites that are both luxurious and stylish, and they all come equipped with modern comforts such as air conditioning, flat-screen TVs, and mini-bars. The suites come along with some supplementary comforts and amenities, such as a separate living area, huge bathrooms, and separate bedrooms.

3. Kempinski Hotel Corvinus

The Kempinski Hotel Corvinus Budapest is a luxurious five-star hotel that can be located in the heart of Budapest, in the nation of Hungary. The hotel's name translates to "Corvinus Kempinski." The hotel offers a one-of-a-kind combination of modern comforts and classic elegance, which is what makes it the perfect location for both business travelers and vacationers seeking a comfortable and convenient place to stay. The hotel offers its visitors a variety of large rooms and suites, all of which are outfitted with enormous windows that provide guests with spectacular views of the surrounding city. The hotel provides guests with several convenient services and facilities, including air conditioning, flat-screen TVs, 24-hour room service, free wireless internet access, a fitness center, and a spa.

The primary restaurant of the hotel is called the Corvinus Restaurant, and it provides guests with a wonderful dining experience with a menu that has a variety of options, including both regional specialties and food from other countries. In addition, the hotel has two bars, a café, a rooftop terrace, and a cigar lounge for guests to select from throughout their stay. The hotel offers its guests a variety of varied chances for recreation, including, among other things, a fitness center, a sauna, and massage services.

4. The Spa at the Anantara New York Palace Hotel

The Anantara New York Palace Budapest is a high-end hotel that has been located in the heart of Budapest and has been awarded five stars for its outstanding service. Because it provides guests with spectacular views of both the city and the Danube River, the Anantara New York Palace Budapest is considered to be one of the most romantic and opulent hotels in the city.

The hotel has a wide variety of luxurious rooms, suites, and apartments, all of which are styled in a modern style and are furnished with contemporary comforts. The hotel also features a contemporary restaurant and bar. The hotel provides its guests with access to a delicious breakfast buffet each morning, and in the evenings, they have a wide variety of options to choose from when it comes to eating at upscale establishments.

The hotel has a broad range of appealing facilities, including an outdoor swimming pool, a fitness center, and a spa, in addition to offering a diverse selection of activities and entertainment alternatives. In addition, guests have the opportunity to relax in the hotel's library, compete with one another in a game of chess, or have a beverage in one of the hotel's two bars.

CHEAP HOTELS IN BUDAPEST

1. The Brody House Hotel

It is generally agreed upon that the Brody House Hotel in Budapest is one of the most outstanding budget hotels in the city. Despite its convenient position in the heart of the city, this hotel offers rooms at prices that won't break the bank while yet maintaining a high standard of comfort. The lodgings are cozy and pleasant, and the staff is kind and eager to assist you in any way they can. There are a variety of rooms accessible to guests at the hotel, including single and double basic rooms, family suites, and even a penthouse. In every one of the rooms, you will find a television, a private bathroom, and a computer with a free wireless internet connection. In addition, the hotel delivers a free breakfast that is of the continental kind to each visitor, and it also has a restaurant that is on the premises and serves Hungarian cuisine in its traditional preparations.

Because of the hotel's excellent position in the middle of the city, it is quite easy for visitors to go to any of the most well-known tourist spots in Budapest. In addition, a good number of the city's most well-known eateries, watering holes, and nightclubs are located within walking distance of the property.

2. Hotel and apartment complex owned by Pal

Pal's Hotel and Apartment is one of the most cost-effective places to stay in Budapest, so vacationers who are searching for a hotel that won't put a strain on their wallets may consider staying at this establishment. The hotel, which can be located in the very heart of the city, is near some of the city's most famous attractions, such as the Chain Bridge, the Hungarian National Museum, and the Hungarian Parliament Building, all of which can be reached on foot.

The hotel gives its guests access to some convenient amenities and services, including a front desk that is manned at all hours of the day and night, a currency exchange, and free Wi-Fi that is available throughout the whole property. In addition, there is a restaurant on the grounds where guests may have a delectable Hungarian meal while they are there. In addition, there is a bar in the hotel that provides guests with access to a comprehensive selection of alcoholic and non-alcoholic drinks.

At Pal's Hotel and Apartment, visitors have the option of unwinding during their stay in one of the hotel's room options, each of which is roomy and well-appointed, and has a private bathroom, air conditioning, and television as standard amenities. Some of the rooms at this establishment have either a balcony or a patio. In addition, the hotel offers a wide range of services to its visitors, such as laundry and ironing, and also makes it possible for them to rent automobiles directly from the establishment. The friendly staff members at Pal's Hotel and Apartment are always happy to be of help, and they are also well-known for providing their clients with great service. The Pal's Hotel and Apartments are a wonderful choice for vacationers who are looking for either a serene setting in which to spend their time or an exciting environment in which to enjoy their time away from home.

3. Kalmár Panzió

It is generally agreed upon that the Kalmár Panzió is one of the most remarkable budget hotels that the city of Budapest has to offer. Because of its position in the center of the city, it offers easy access to a number of the city's most well-known tourist attractions, such as the Hungarian Parliament Building, Buda Castle, the Széchenyi Thermal Bath, and a lot of other attractions as well. The hotel provides guests with a broad range of amenities, including free WiFi, an on-site restaurant, a fitness center, and a sauna. Additionally, the hotel is pet-friendly. The rooms have a modern aesthetic, are fitted with air conditioning and flat-screen TVs, and have a contemporary style. They are comfortable and spacious. The staff members are kind and inviting, and they provide exceptional service to the patrons of the establishment. In addition, the hotel offers a variety of vacation packages, some of which include guided tours of the city in addition to services provided by the spa and other attractions. Because of all of these qualities, the Kalmár Panzió is a good option for travelers who are looking for a place to stay in Budapest that is on the more affordable side of things.

4. The Magazine Hotel and Apartments

The Magazine Hotel and Apartment is often regarded as among the most highly recommended low-cost hotels in Budapest, and its rankings reflect this reputation. It is a wonderful place to stay for travelers who are interested in visiting the city due to its location in the center of the city and its proximity to the famous Chain Bridge. The hotel provides its guests with a broad range of lodging options to choose from, including suites, apartments, and the more traditional single and double guest rooms. All of the rooms have a modern design and are completely outfitted with amenities such as air conditioning and free wireless internet connection. In addition, the hotel offers a broad variety of services, some of which include a currency exchange, a luggage storage room, a laundry service, and a reception desk that is manned around the clock.

For visitors looking for a comfortable place to stay without breaking the bank, the Magazine Hotel and Apartment is an excellent choice. Because the accommodation rates are so affordable, it is a good option for tourists who want to cut down on the amount of money they spend while they are in Budapest. Because of its convenient position, the hotel is close to both the most popular attractions in the city as well as public transportation, making it quite easy to go about the rest of the city. In addition, the hotel offers guests a diverse selection of activities and services, making it possible for them to have an enjoyable time throughout their whole stay at the establishment.

The Magazine Hotel and Apartment is an ideal solution for tourists on a limited budget who are interested in staying in the Budapest region. If you are one of these tourists, you should consider staying at the Magazine Hotel and Apartment. It is priced in a manner that makes it relatively inexpensive despite its amazing facilities, its location, which is pretty lovely, and its assortment of wonderful amenities. The Magazine Hotel and Apartment is one of the most sought-after alternatives for housing in Budapest as a result of the competitive hotel rates, cutting-edge facilities, and friendly service it provides.

CHAPTER 3

HOW TO MOVE AROUND IN AND AROUND BUDAPEST

The city of Budapest is a wonderful destination for sightseeing. From the UNESCO World Heritage Site that is Castle Hill to the magnificent sweep of the Grand Boulevard, this lovely city in central Europe is regarded for being one of the most attractive in all of continental Europe.

When navigating Budapest, you must keep in mind that the city is comprised of two separate cities. First, there's Buda, which is where Castle Hill and the rest of the Buda Hills are located. Pest is located on the other bank of the river, and it is in this neighborhood that the majority of the city's pubs, restaurants, and other services can be found. There is an extensive network of public transportation in Budapest that links the two halves of the city. This network includes trains, Metro lines, streetcars, and a variety of other modes of conveyance to facilitate simpler movement within the city. And if you find yourself out enjoying some of the must-do things to do in Budapest at night, such as visiting the city's famed ruin pubs, you'll be happy to hear that Budapest offers decent night bus services that make it simple to get about the city.

However, before you start exploring the public transportation system of the city, you should be sure to drop off your baggage at the Bounce luggage storage facility in Budapest. Because crowded trams and trains are not the places for carrying big baggage, you may make it simpler to navigate Budapest by leaving your luggage behind at a secure location with Bounce.

How to navigate Budapest with the rail system

Although it is not the only one, Keleti Station is the most important train terminal in Budapest, which is the Hungarian capital. Keleti is Budapest's Eastern train station, whereas Nyugati Pályaudvar is the city's Western train station, and Déli Pályaudvar is the city's Southern train station. These stations get train traffic from all around Hungary as well as from many other countries in Europe. The Keleti train station, which is located in the eastern part of the city, provides links to the Balkans and the rest of Eastern Europe. On the other hand, the Western railway station provides connections to Vienna, Paris, and other towns to the west. However, 36 of the 53 intercity train routes to Budapest stop at Keleti station, which means there is a considerable probability that you may find yourself here at some point.

Fortunately, all of Budapest's railway stations are well-connected to the public transportation network of the city. This makes it simple to go to the city center or just about anyplace else you need to go by using a combination of Metro lines, the tram line, or by taking a bus.

Ferenc Liszt International Airport is the most likely location for your arrival if you want to go to the city by airplane. This airport serves as the primary aviation hub for the city and is also the biggest airport in Hungary. Regrettably, there is no direct rail connection between the airport and the city at this time; however, a high-speed route to the Keleti station has been planned. At this time, you will need to go to the Ferighey railway station using bus 200E. Nearly one hundred trains a day leave from there for the Nyugati Station, and the trip takes approximately a quarter of an hour. This station is conveniently situated near the heart of the city, providing easy access to the city's extensive public transportation system. A minibus shuttle or bus

100E, which travels directly between the airport and the city center of Budapest, are two more options for getting from the Budapest airport into the city.

The Metro is your best bet for getting about Budapest.

The metro system in Budapest is virtually an attraction unto itself in its own right. After London, Budapest became the second city in the world to establish an underground metro system.

London was the first. However, although most people wouldn't call the London Underground especially lovely, you can't deny that the Budapest Metro stations are stunning. A journey on the Budapest Metro might give the impression of traveling back in time because the stations on Metro Line 1 have been maintained and appear largely the same as they did when they originally opened in 1896.

There are four distinct Metro lines in Budapest, each of which is denoted by a number as well as a color. Because it links many of the most popular tourist destinations on the Pest side of the city, Metro Line 1 (also known as the Yellow Line) was the first subway line in the city and is still considered to be the one that is likely to be of the greatest benefit to tourists. In the middle to late part of the 20th century, more lines were added. Line 2, popularly known as the Red Line, travels through the heart of the city and links Pest and Buda. Line 3, often known as the Blue Line, remains on the Pest side of the river the whole time it travels in a generally north-south direction, linking the city's most remote neighborhoods. In conclusion, Green Line 4 is the only one of the city's subway lines that travels over the river to the south.

A valid ticket is required to ride any of the lines that make up the Budapest Metro. Inside the Metro station, you will find the option to buy individual tickets. You have to use one of the orange machines that are located close to the platform to verify that your ticket is valid. Only then may you board the train. If you travel without first having your ticket validated, you will be considered to have traveled without a ticket at all, which might result in a hefty punishment. Because a single ticket only allows for travel on a single Metro line for a total of eighty minutes, you will need to purchase an additional ticket if you wish to switch lines. During the evening, a single ticket is valid for one hour and twenty minutes of public transit.

The BKK, which is the same Budapest transport business that manages all of the city's public transport infrastructure, is the entity in charge of operating the Metro. As a result, it is possible tram routes and directions for getting around Budapest

In addition, there is a network of ancient trams that runs across Budapest. It is still one of the biggest tram networks in the world, even though it has been a part of the city since 1866, making it the predecessor of the Metro system. 38

separate lines make up the tram network, in addition to a cogwheel railway, which means that there is almost no part of the city that is not accessible by the streetcars. Be aware, however, that some lines, particularly those in the city center, have the potential to get very crowded, particularly at the busiest periods of the day. Remember that these lines are not just utilized by tourists, but also heavily used by residents as a means to commute to and from work, and act appropriately while using public transportation as a result. Tram line 2 is particularly remarkable because it offers spectacular views of Buda Castle and the Buda Hills as it travels along the Pest side of the Danube River. This route may be found on the Pest side of the river. Instead of focusing on getting somewhere specific, it could be more beneficial to take advantage of this tram's low cost and ride it as a sort of inexpensive sightseeing.

How to navigate around Budapest with the public bus system

It is to be expected that a contemporary capital city such as Budapest would have an extensive network of bus lines that operate both during the day and at night. Unlike in some other cities, you won't be able to buy tickets as you board the bus in this one; instead, you'll need to utilize one of the ticket machines or buy them from a newspaper kiosk before boarding the bus. Buying a transit pass rather than individual tickets is the easiest method to ensure that you will never be caught without a ticket while using public transportation.

When the sun goes dark in Budapest, the bus network comes into its own and shines brightly. After all, Budapest is a great place to go out and party, and its nightlife is often considered to be among the liveliest in all of Europe. Because Budapest's night buses operate on 41 different lines and continue into the wee hours of the morning, you should never find yourself stuck with no other option but to call one of the city's taxi drivers for assistance. Tram line 6 runs throughout the night, making it a convenient option to travel back to your lodgings after spending the evening at one of Budapest's many busy bars or pubs.

Driving directions for getting around Budapest

Budapest, like many other cities that were constructed before the invention of vehicles, is not truly planned for mobility by the car. This is particularly the case in the heart of the city. The infrastructure in the central part of Budapest is not geared for driving, in contrast to the surrounding suburbs, which have excellent highway links to contemporary roadways. You should anticipate small streets that have a lot of obscure laws and a severe shortage of parking places.

A vehicle is probably a sensible investment if you have plans to go to the outskirts of the city to investigate other neighborhoods. However, if you can do so, you should try to avoid driving in the central business district of the city. Because Budapest's public transportation system is so comprehensive, not to mention reasonably priced and user-friendly, it is often preferable to depend on it rather than attempt to drive and subject oneself to the associated stress.

Driving directions for getting around Budapest

Budapest, like many other cities that were constructed before the invention of vehicles, is not truly planned for mobility by the car. This is particularly the case in the heart of the city. The infrastructure in the central part of Budapest is not geared for driving, in contrast to the surrounding suburbs, which have excellent highway links to contemporary roadways. You should anticipate small streets that have a lot of obscure laws and a severe shortage of parking places.

A vehicle is probably a sensible investment if you have plans to go to the outskirts of the city to investigate other neighborhoods. However, if you can do so, you should try to avoid driving in the central business district of the city. Because Budapest's public transportation system is so comprehensive, not to mention reasonably priced and user-friendly, it is often preferable to depend on it rather than attempt to drive and subject oneself to the associated stress.

Is it possible to walk around all of Budapest?
The city of Budapest is rather sizable. On the other hand, many of the city's most popular attractions and neighborhoods are located near one another and the central business district. As a result, exploring the city on foot is often the most effective method to take advantage of all it has to offer. By strolling around the city, not

only will you be able to get some exercise but you'll also be able to take in the magnificent architecture and be open to making some unanticipated discoveries. And even if you do manage to wear yourself out, Budapest's extensive public transportation system is never too far away, so you can always take a break from walking by hopping on a metro train, a tram, or a bus at any time.

While the Buda side of the city has more rolling hills, the Pest side of the city is quite flat. If the idea of walking does not appeal to you, another option is to think about renting a bicycle. You may move about Budapest quickly and securely on one of the city's many bike lanes, which will allow you to see more sights in a shorter amount of time.

Budapest Travel Guide

CHAPTER 4

BEST SHOPPING LOCATIONS IN BUDAPEST

The greatest locations to shop in Budapest are located along pedestrian-only strips and inside large plazas on the outskirts of the city. These are the most convenient areas to shop. When you visit this magical city, you won't have any trouble locating the ideal place to go shopping at any time throughout your trip.

With its lovely age-old alleyways that are bursting with trendsetting shops and enormous shopping complexes, Budapest is one of the greatest shopping destinations in Europe. Budapest is one of the best shopping destinations in Europe. The city offers a dizzying array of shopping opportunities, whether your idea of a good time is perusing tempting old jewels or well-known worldwide names. In addition, there is usually a nice restaurant or café close by in case you feel the need to take a break at any point throughout the day.

1. Vaci Street

Vaci strip is the premier pedestrian shopping strip in Budapest, and each side of this lively attraction has an abundance of restaurants, cafes, and shops selling a variety of goods. The route covers a distance of more than one kilometer before terminating at the Central Market Hall, and it begins in the heart of Budapest at the historic Vorosmarty Square.

Along the route, there is no lack of souvenir shops where you may buy something unique to take back with you to remember your trip. In addition, there are a ton of fantastic retail buying opportunities, such as Zara, Flying Tiger Copenhagen, and Adidas, which ensures that you will be able to locate the most up-to-date clothing and homewares to pack in your baggage.

2. Markets in Budapest

The enormous markets in Budapest are one of the city's most famous attractions. These markets sell almost everything, from locally made clothing and accessories to mouthwatering farm-to-table cuisine. The Central Market Hall is often considered to be the most famous location in the city for those in search of superb food. This enormous indoor bazaar, which opened in 1897 and covers three stories, is home to almost every delectable treat that can be imagined.

When in search of low-key activity, the Ecseri Flea Market is an excellent place to stop. In this place, you will find a plethora of unique pieces of furniture, homewares, and antique treasures, and the majority of these items come with an interesting backstory. Finally, the renowned Budapest Christmas Market can be found at Vorosmarty Square. This market has one hundred unique vendors that are sure to keep visitors entertained for hours.

3. Place d'Haute Couture

Fashion Although it just only a few blocks, the Street is packed to the brim with high-end apparel boutiques that can elevate your look to the next level. You are free to stroll the pavement while you go about window shopping before deciding on a store to investigate more inside due to the design that restricts vehicular traffic to pedestrians only.

Given the name of the city, it should come as no surprise that this location is home to a significant number of the most successful fashion businesses in the world. Lacoste, Tommy Hilfiger, Cos, and Philipp Plein are just a few examples of well-known labels. Some lavish hotels, such as The Ritz-Carlton Budapest, are also home to businesses selling high-end home furnishings and accessories.

4. Andrássy Avenue

Andrássy Avenue is the place to go if you want to find some of the most recognizable fashion names in the world. It passes through the heart of Budapest's historic center while being bordered on both sides by tree-lined streets. You will be able to browse for luxury labels such as Gucci, Burberry, Louis Vuitton, and The North Face, amongst a great many more.

Make sure to set aside some time to explore the cultural pleasures that are on show while you are visiting this incredible shopping destination. These cultural delights range from the opulent

Museum of Fine Arts to the ultra-modern Q Contemporary. Andrássy Avenue is the place to go to get a taste of the most enticing aspects of Budapest's culture and way of life.

5. Falk Miksa Street

On Falk Miksa Street, you'll find a concentration of some of the most well-regarded antique stores in all of Budapest. However, you shouldn't be shocked if you can't find a good deal at any of these places since many of them cater to wealthy customers who are wanting to purchase unique items of furniture, silverware, and jewelry.

Visit some of Budapest's most interesting museums and galleries while you're in this section of the city to make the most of your time there. If you are interested in participating in an expensive bidding competition, the Kieselbach Gallery often holds art auctions in addition to a wide variety of contemporary art exhibits.

6. Retrock Designer Vintage Store

Those who are interested in adorning themselves in fashionable styles from the past will find that Retrock Designer Vintage Store is an excellent choice. Since the international culture that Budapest provides ensures that many of the city's citizens are undoubtedly stylish, Budapest is the place to go to discover some high-quality vintage gear that will set you apart from the crowd.

Many of the objects on show are stunning pieces that were manufactured by well-known brands but were simply forgotten about in someone's closet for far too long. The exhibition is spread out over two very crowded floors. You may get a fantastic price by browsing the various racks that are stocked at Retrock Designer Vintage Store.

7. The shopping center in West End

The Westend Shopping Center is widely regarded as one of the best places to shop in all of Budapest. The building complex has three expansive rooftop gardens that look out over the posh neighborhood of Terézváros.

It is recommended that a few hours be set aside to visit the more than 400 shops that are included inside the complex. Those interested in fashion will be able to locate popular labels such as Nike, Orsay, Columbia, and Superdry. In the meanwhile, there are also fifty different restaurants and places to dine available for when your feet need a break. TGI Fridays, Okay Italia, and Bellozzo are three excellent restaurants where you may have a mouthwatering supper.

8. Arena Mall

The enormous retail shopping center known as Arena Mall is home to several of the most well-known brands in the world, including Calvin Klein, Armani, Desigual, and Levi's, amongst others. This shopping center is fantastic for tourists who want to make the most of their time in Budapest since they can get everything they want in a single location here.

In addition to these shopping behemoths, Cinema City offers visually stunning IMAX screenings that you shouldn't miss. It is possible to spend the whole day wandering this enormous complex before eventually recovering your breath with an amusing film since the most recent blockbuster movies are played late into the evening. This makes it simple to spend the day.

9. Paloma Budapest

Paloma Discovering many of Hungary's most fascinating up-and-coming designers and artists is made much easier by the city of Budapest. This hip location is housed inside a historic structure that dates back to the 19th century and had previously fallen into ruin. Since the proprietors took over the space in 2014, more than 40 local creatives have made it their home.

You'll discover enormously talented artisans making anything from high-end leather products and jewelry to ethical apparel and clothing made from sustainable materials inside towering archways and ringing a delightful internal courtyard. Make plans to stop by Paloma to get a glimpse of the work being produced by Budapest's up-and-coming artists and designers.

BEST BUDAPEST NIGHTLIFE

The nightlife of Budapest will treat you like royalty and provide you with an evening you won't soon forget. It is the "Ruin Bars" in this nation's capital that set it distinct from the other locations in the country and made the nightlife there an unforgettable adventure. The greatest nightclubs in Budapest are known for providing patrons with an evening that is filled with sparkle and elegance. Include these clubs on your itinerary if you want to feel immersed in the energetic atmosphere of the location. The city of Budapest is home to a large number of nightclubs and ruin bars, providing a diverse array of options for those who like going out to clubs to drink and dance to the sounds of the music. Check out these nightclubs and experience the finest of Budapest's nightlife while you are in the nation's capital city. If you are unsure where you should go when you are in the country's capital city.

1. Akvarium Club

The Akvarium Club is a charming venue where one can have a wonderful time after dark and is widely regarded as one of the most popular nightclubs in Budapest. This major nightclub plays home to a wide variety of performances regularly, which makes it an enticing draw for those who like going out to parties. It has a stylish and well-designed center area where guests may sit and relax while listening to the music beats, and its wonderfully illuminated terrace is certainly a pleasure for guests. This venue may be found in the heart of Budapest's renowned party district.

2. The Corvin Club, Including Its Rooftop Terrace

The Corvin Club, which is located in an ancient Soviet block and is located above a supermarket, exudes a highly distinct and one-of-a-kind atmosphere throughout its interiors, which places it on the list of the top clubs in Budapest. In contrast to the other watering holes in town, this club has doors that intertwine with one another as well as a rooftop bar with a panoramic view of the city of Budapest below. This club is a good example of the more low-key side of the nightlife in Budapest since it does not include the typical techno music that is played there.

3. Mazel Tov

If you are looking for a romantic dinner spot in Budapest, then you could find yourself at Mazel

Tov at some point in your hunt. This establishment, which has a fashionable and roomy atmosphere, is a lively participant in the nighttime scene. After a long and stressful day, you may unwind at this venue thanks to its enormous courtyard, which functions as a multicultural space and is decked with trees and fairy lights. In addition to this, it will most certainly provide you with some gorgeous corners that you may use for your Instagram feed. This establishment receives a particular mention in the nightlife guide for Budapest.

4. Racskert

Can you see yourself bopping to the rhythms and having a good time in a parking lot? Naturally, it's very intriguing to think about it, but Racskert will provide you the opportunity to experience Budapest nightlife at its finest, and that too in a vehicle parking lot that has been transformed into a nightclub. The nightclub's interior design exudes a joyous spirit, and the graffiti-covered walls contribute to the establishment's allure. It is one of the locals' favorite party spots since it is inexpensive yet offers a wide selection of excellent drinks and delectable cuisine.

5. 360 Bar

When you visit this enticing rooftop restaurant in the nation's capital, you will be able to get a look at the breathtaking panorama that encompasses the whole city, which is where the restaurant got its name. This dining establishment not only has an extravagant and scenic view, but it also provides a scrumptious variety of meals and an enormous wine list. Therefore, if you find yourself in the city and are interested in having a few drinks while taking in a breathtaking view, then this establishment should be at the top of your list for experiencing the nightlife in Budapest, Hungary at its very finest.

6. Otkert Club

The Otkert club, which was established in a structure that was constructed in the 19th century, gives the nightlife in Budapest an edge. This nightclub is situated in the heart of the city and offers a refined party experience among the beautifully restored ruins. This popular party spot holds a wide variety of themed events during the majority of the summer evenings, and it also welcomes a large number of prominent DJs that get partygoers moving to the rhythms.

7. FogasHaz

Fogas Haz, which underwent extensive renovations in 2010, has established itself as the go-to party spot for tourists who are interested in experiencing the most exciting aspects of Budapest's nightlife. This establishment, which is widely regarded as one of the forefathers of the ruined bar scene, will allow you to get captivated by its vivid atmosphere and brightly colored décor. In addition to an open dance floor, a thrift store, and a martini terrace bar, it also functions as a cultural art center and bar.

8. Sparty

Sparty is a nightclub in Budapest that has brightly illuminated dance floors, loud music, and access to the city's therapeutic springs. The weekend night parties that are all the rage are not only popular among visitors but also among residents, who are looking forward to the night event. A result of this is that the nightlife in the nation's capital has taken on an entirely new feel as a result of its exciting environment and novel idea.

9. Kobuci

This nightclub may be found in a neighborhood known as Obuda, which is somewhat far from the city's busiest thoroughfares. Kobuci is separated from the commotion of the surrounding area and has the air of a hidden garden thanks to the fact that it is enclosed inside a courtyard and is encircled by a row of trees. Although it is not a nightclub, this venue is well-known for organizing events at which DJs and musicians gather to perform late into the night.

10. Doboz

As soon as you enter this eccentric nightclub in Budapest, you will be captivated by the sights that greet you on the premises. The layout of the nightclub was thoughtfully planned so that patrons would get the impression they were wandering through a labyrinth that led them to the main area of the establishment. with a combination of music that grooves and bright lights. In addition, throughout the warm months, this hip nightclub throws outdoor parties in the space behind the club in its garden.

FUN FACTS ABOUT BUDAPEST

Fun Facts About Budapest You Probably Didn't Know That You Need to Put Budapest on Your Travel Bucket List! This city is just begging to be explored since it is teeming with amazing art, historical sites, thermal baths, wonderful marketplaces, pubs, and restaurants. We are going to provide you with the most intriguing and entertaining fun facts about Budapest, which will increase your desire to visit this city.

1. Budapest Was Established by the Original Three Cities

The three cities of Buda, Pest, and Buda were merged into one in 1873 to create Budapest, which is now the capital of Hungary. Today, Buda is often linked with affluent neighborhoods and the high class, while Pest is where you will find the majority of the people and what is traditionally understood to be "urban living." The majestic bridge of Széchenyi, sometimes referred to as the "Chain Bridge," links the two cities of Buda and Pest.

2. Budapest is widely regarded as the Spa Industry's Mecca Throughout the World

Because of the vast amount of spring water that is stored underneath the city and the daily production of 70 million liters of thermal water, Budapest is considered to be the city in the world that has the richest supply of medicinal water. Not only are there healing spas in Budapest but there are also pool parties that go on late into the night. Gellért, Rudas, Széchenyi, Lukács, and Király are some of the most beautiful spas in Hungary, and you should go to all of them.

3. Hippos at the Budapest Zoo Are Enjoying the Thermal Waters as They Soak

The water that is used in the pool that is designated for the hippos at the Budapest Zoo originates from the spring that is located inside Széchenyi Thermal Bath. Due to the fact that the composition of the artesian water is relatively similar to that of the waters of the Nile, it has a good impact on these hippos.

4. It is quite challenging to become fluent in the Hungarian language.

One of the toughest languages in the world to pick up is Hungarian, which is a member of the Finno-Ugrian language family and is in the top 10 most difficult languages to learn. Here are three "easy" terms that you should try to memorize before your next trip to Budapest:

1. *Hi -> Szia*
2. *Thanks -> Köszönöm*
3. *Cheers -> Egészségedre*

5. The largest synagogue in all of Europe is located in Budapest.

The synagogue on Dohány Street, usually referred to as the Great Synagogue, is widely regarded as one of the most magnificent places of prayer in all of Budapest and is an absolute must-see. It includes design elements that are reminiscent of Moorish, Byzantine, Romantic, and even Gothic, giving it a mystifying atmosphere within.

6. The law places restrictions on the use of Hungarian names.

When it comes to deciding what to call their offspring, parents in Hungary are subject to the country's naming regulations. The name has to come from a list that has been pre-approved, and any variations from that list have to be submitted to the Research Institute for Linguistics of the Hungarian Academy of Sciences for review and approval. There are no Brooklyn or Norths there.

7. Budapest's public transportation system is the oldest in all of continental Europe.

After the London Underground, the Budapest Millennium subterranean line is the second oldest underground line in Europe (after the London Underground), but it is the first subterranean line in continental Europe. It opened in 1896. The subway system in Budapest is the only one of its kind in the whole world to be recognized as a World Heritage Site by UNESCO.

CHAPTERS 5

TRAVELING ESSENTIALS

What kinds of things should I take with me when I go into the city?

Carry-on baggage is the most practical choice for short journeys inside a city since it can be easily stored and transported. Before you get on the aircraft, you should make it a habit to double-check the carry-on baggage restrictions that are imposed by the airline you are flying with.

When you embark on a vacation to the city, the only things you are required to carry with you are the bare necessities; hence, this is the category in which you should concentrate your packing efforts. The following items need to be included in your packing list if you will be traveling with just carry-on baggage:

- Vanity bag constructed of a see-through material (which is essential for going past security checks at airports).
- Shower gel
- Included in this package are both a toothbrush and toothpaste.
- If the amount of creams, gels, and other forms of personal cosmetics you are using is less than one hundred milliliters, place them all in a transparent bag.
- When traveling during the warmer months, it is important to have sunscreen with you.
- Ibuprofen and aspirin are the best treatments for headaches; everything else

you need may be purchased after you reach your destination.
- Earplugs and a sleeping mask are items that you should carry along with you on a trip to the city just in case you have problems falling asleep in strange situations or when traveling.

- The essentials you need for the winter vacations
- Keep in mind the most important things, and store them in a safe place; criminals gravitate toward major cities because of the abundance of possibilities for theft that can be found there.

- ID / Passport
- Funds denominated in the nation's currency that is used there (the majority of

the time, currency exchange offices may be found at airports).
- When traveling internationally, withdrawing cash with a credit card is a convenient option.
- information printed out regarding lodgings, including addresses (you may also store them on your phone if you like).
- Those who are planning to travel outside of their country should seriously consider purchasing travel health insurance.

In preparation for a quick journey into the city, what essentials should you include in your bag?

If you are only going to be in a place for one night, all you need to carry with you is a change of clothes in addition to the basics like toothpaste, a toothbrush, shampoo, and soap.

This allows you to minimize the number of belongings that you bring with you when you travel.

What should you pack for a journey that will take you throughout the city for four days?

It is feasible to go to a place for forty nights by just bringing a relatively small piece of luggage with you; nevertheless, you will almost surely need extra clothing, especially when traveling during the winter months. in addition to essentials such as toothpaste, a toothbrush, shampoo, soap, and a clean pair of clothing to wear.

Places of interest for tourists located in and around the city

A City Break is the perfect way to take the opportunity of national vacation such as when you've got either Monday, Thursday, or Friday off, and it also means that you have the option to go for an even longer weekend if you so choose. This kind of vacation is also an excellent way to take advantage of free time when you do not have a holiday. A shorter version of a typical vacation, also often called a "mini" vacation. Because airlines may charge higher fares for certain days, you should make every effort to book your flight in advance to take advantage of any deals that could be available. Investigate the idea of making use of one of the many alternative options that are accessible, such as an inexpensive bus service or train travel. There are a lot of different possibilities.

Vacations in Budapest, the Capital of Hungary

If you want your weekend trip to be one that you will always remember, a visit to Budapest is an essential need. Budapest, the nation's capital, has consistently ranked among the "Top Ten Cities in the World to Visit" list for a considerable amount of time. It should not come as a surprise that this lovely city, which is situated in the very heart of Europe, is a popular holiday place for a substantial number of visitors from all over Europe who come from all over Europe. Its one-of-a-kind architecture, stunning monuments, vibrant cultural life, exceptional food, and world-famous spas are certain to win you over.

THE BEST OF FESTIVALS IN BUDAPEST

There is no question that Budapest is a destination that every person should go to at least once in their lifetime. Whether you are interested in unwinding in one of the well-known thermal baths that are spread out across the city, going on a pub crawl through the well-known ruins pubs, or taking in the views from one of the city's key vantage points, there is no question that Budapest is a place that everyone should visit.

Festivals in Budapest are so amazing that they should be on everyone's list of things to do at least once in their lives. This is especially true for those who live for the party scene. Throughout the height of the summer, Hungary plays home to a myriad of excellent music festivals in addition to other traditional cultural events that are guaranteed to make just about everyone happy.

1. Sziget Festival

The Sziget Festival is one of the biggest music festivals in the world, and it takes place in Budapest. The festival showcases performances from a wide range of musical genres. Since its debut in 1993, only a short time after the fall of the Soviet Union, the festival has never taken a break from its continuous schedule of events.

Sziget is regarded to be one of the festivals that should be on everyone's radar since it attracts over 600,000 people every year and has a roster that includes some of the most well-known personalities in the music industry. The Sziget music festival transforms Obuda Island into a fully operational musical haven.

The distinctiveness of this festival may be attributed to the wide variety of activities that are offered in addition to the music. There are dance stages, a cinema, a theater, performances of contemporary circus, sports events, and even a beach where you can swim in the Danube. All of these things may be found at the Danube Spring Festival. In addition to the music, all of these other activities will also be available.

2. The Telekom Volt Festival

It is widely acknowledged that the VOLT Festival, which takes place annually in Sopron, is one of the major music events that take place throughout the whole of Hungary. Since 1993, the festival has been conducted every year, and its name comes from a journal that is dedicated to popular culture and has the same name.

As part of VOLT's cooperation with Sziget, which will result in the two festivals becoming siblings, VOLT will be presenting a roster that encompasses all musical genres, including electronic, rock, pop, jazz, and urban music. This roster will include a wide variety of musical acts. But of course, any festival that is regarded to be of world-class rank is about more than just music, and Volt is no exception; it offers theatrical performances, visual art exhibitions, film screenings, and screenings of sporting events, among other things. Volt is an exception to the rule.

3. The Festival of the Sound of Balaton

The events in the book Balaton Sound take place around the gorgeous Lake Balaton in Hungary, which acts as the background for the story. The festival that is the sibling of Sziget is now in its second decade, and it is acknowledged for placing Hungary on the map in terms of being an essential location for the most premium summer beach festival experience there is to be had.

As you can spend your days either dancing at boat parties, chilling out at the nearby food and drink spots, or sunbathing lakeside and truly making the most of the beautiful weather, what better soundtrack do you need than impressive lineups featuring the world's best electronic dance music (EDM), house, and hip-hop artists performing across nine stages? What better way to make the most of the wonderful weather?

When the party is as wonderful as it is at Balaton Sound, why wouldn't you want to be there? People travel from all over Europe to be a part of it, and it's simple to see why.

4. Bánkitó Festival

During the Bánkitó Festival, which takes place in Bánk, Hungary, alternative music is given a platform to be performed. The event is a bastion of innovation and unconstrained ideas due to its fiercely independent character. Bánkitó attracts an educated and loyal audience by curating a lineup of musical performers from a broad range of genres who all share a love for the role that the artist plays in society. This enthusiasm for the artist's role in society is a driving force behind the festival. Every year, the festival selects a fresh theme and zeroes in on that topic across all of its presentations, both artistic and intellectual.

5. EFOTT Festival

The EFOTT event is a music event that takes place in Velence, Hungary and offers a range of musical genres as its performers. The event, which takes place near Lake Velence, is an example of a typical summer holiday location. The festival is the Hungarian equivalent of Spring Break in the United States, and it brings together around one hundred thousand students each year to celebrate the successful conclusion of another cycle of tests. In the United States, Spring Break is celebrated during the first full week of April. The festival offers a broad mix of chart-toppers on seven stages throughout the entirety of its four days of operation. An extensive roster has been compiled for the event. However, EFOTT is not just a party since, for years, the festival's organizers have been spending a lot of effort on enhancing the cultural and athletic lifestyles of the students in addition to the musical activities. As a consequence, the festival has continuously broken attendance records, which is one reason why EFOTT is not just a party. Because of this, the daytime programs are expanding almost every year, and not only in terms of the number of personnel; they are also improving in terms of the quality of the services that they provide. One of the key goals of EFOTT is to make it possible for participants to take advantage of a waterfront vacation while they are attending the festival. This is in addition to the fact that one of the primary goals of EFOTT is to provide attendees with constant entertainment.

6. Veszprémfest

Veszprémfest is a large-scale cultural event that has been going on for fifteen years, is increasing at a quick rate, and is providing true value for art and music aficionados living in Veszprém and all across the country. The festival takes place for several days throughout the summer months every year, and it features performances by some of the most brilliant and renowned musicians in the world, hailing from a wide range of musical subgenres, such as classical music, world music, opera, jazz, or pop music.

7. Festival Of Folk Arts BUDAPEST

You should go to the Festival of Folk Arts in Budapest's Castle District if you are interested in learning more about the many folklore and crafts that are practiced in nations all over the world, including Hungary. There, you will have the opportunity to have conversations with the individuals that carry out these customs. The Folk Festival, which is now being held for the

32nd time, is the most significant venue in Hungary for the preservation of live folk culture. Local artists and craftsmen from different sections of the country, including some of the most well-known in their specialties, will impart the information and skills that have been handed down from generation to generation.

8. The Festival of Christmas Markets in Budapest

Visit the Budapest Christmas Fair and Winter Festival in Vorosmarty Square if you are looking for one-of-a-kind and exceptional presents to offer to the people in your life. You will find a wide variety of unique and one-of-a-kind items there. The gorgeous plaza that can be found in the center of the city is converted into a bustling market beginning in early November and lasting until early January.

The location of the Square could not be handier; it is located at the very end of Váci utca, in the very heart of the city, and directly in front of the well-known Gerbeaud Coffee House. One of the most scenic spots in Budapest is converted into a winter market in the two weeks leading up to the winter holidays by the erection of stalls made of wood that have a rustic appearance and two outdoor stages.

9. The Spring Festival in Budapest

The Spring Festival in Budapest is a cultural event that takes place over around four weeks and spans a total of forty various places across the city. It contains a total of 120 distinct activities. The varied calendar includes performances of opera, ballet, chamber music, jazz, and exhibitions, as well as a large number of events that do not cost anything to participate in. Every year, it is considered to be one of the most important cultural festivals in Europe, and it showcases a diverse array of artists from all over the world.

The 39th annual Budapest Spring Festival will welcome attendees with a program that showcases a diverse range of creative expressions from all around the world. Activities in the realms of classical music, opera, jazz, world music, dance, contemporary circus, theater, and the visual arts are some of the things that guests may look forward to participating in. The Budapest Spring Festival is an unusual event that combines various organizations and shows works that are making their global debut for the first time. It showcases the most creative artists from Hungary as well as artists from other countries and regions throughout the world.

10. The Jewish Festival of the Summer

The Jewish Summer Festival is held in a city that has a significant amount of Jewish history and heritage, and the synagogue that serves as the festival's centerpiece is one of the most gorgeous buildings on the continent. The Great Synagogue on Dohány Street, which is the second biggest in the world, and the Rumbach Street Synagogue will both host performances of Jewish music during the week. These performances will range from klezmer and string quartets to fusion jazz and pipe organ. These performances will be available for the participants to see and enjoy.

11. BUDAPEST Summer Festival

The ongoing summer cultural festival in Budapest is now presenting a broad range of open-air summer evening entertainment, ranging from opera performances and puppet shows to classical concerts and circus acts. These summer evening events take place at the city's Margaret Island Park. There is a diverse selection of places to visit, the majority of which are situated in areas of the city that receive more breeze. These areas of the city offer some cool options for amusing oneself in greener surroundings during the warmer months of the year, such as the picturesque Margaret Island or the pleasant Varosmajor Park on the Buda side of Budapest. There is a diverse selection of places to visit, the majority of which are situated in more breezy regions of the city.

MONTH BY MONTH IN BUDAPEST

January

People who wish to do a lot of sightseeing in Budapest should probably avoid the month of January since it is the coldest month of the year there and because the weather is not great during this time of year. This is because January is the coldest month of the year there. If, on the other hand, you are the kind of person who savors the experience of snow, then this location is a veritable paradise for you. There is a substantial quantity of snow that has fallen throughout the whole of Budapest, and there is a range of activities that may be carried out in the snow.

One of these activities is sledding. You could go to the City Park Ice Rink and give ice skating a go, or you could toboggan down the Buda Hills. Both options are available to you. You will always have access to these activities. You might also have a wonderful time at the local dance house by going there and dancing to some traditional Hungarian music. January is the month when both the theatrical and opera seasons reach their pinnacle points.

February

Even if it does not become quite as cold as it does in December and January, February is still regarded to be a winter month, and the temperature is perfect for sipping mulled wine and eating traditional, "heavier" Hungarian delicacies like burka, which is a sort of blood sausage. Throughout February, there are several different artisan fairs and gastronomic festivals take place. Festivals such as the one celebrating fish and the one celebrating Mangalica are two examples of this kind of festivities. If you and your significant other are planning to take a trip around the time of Valentine's Day, Budapest is a fantastic option for you to take into consideration as a potential holiday spot. You have the choice of going on a romantic dinner cruise down the Danube or going on a weekend getaway to one of the resorts in the Buda Hills. Both of these options are available to you.

March

During March, a discernible change in the weather is likely to occur as a result of the seasonal transition from winter to spring. The first few days of better weather have generated a general increase in activity and discussion throughout the whole city, and both inhabitants of the city and tourists to the city are starting to venture out into the city in larger numbers. This might be because more people are walking about the city. When the weather starts to turn a little chillier, museums, theaters, and art galleries are still great places to go. On the other hand, if you want to spend the day basking in the pre-summer sun, you may visit outdoor attractions such as the Budapest Zoo and the Botanical Garden. The Hungarian city observes Memorial Day, which takes place on March 15th, as a means to remember the revolution that took place in Hungary in the year 1848.

April

April is the month when spring is in full swing, with brilliant colors emerging everywhere, flowers starting to open, a proliferation of spring festivals, and a broad range of activities that may be done outdoors. Attend the Cherry Blossom Festival to see the splendor and grandeur of the European spring, or go to the Japanese Garden on Margaret Island to observe the flowering of spring. Both of these events can be found on the island. These two sites are both considered to be in Europe. You may also get the full Hungarian experience by participating in the Easter celebrations and rituals that are held around this occasion, such as decorating eggs. These traditions are a big part of Hungarian culture. There is no need for you to be afraid about the city being overrun with tourists during April since April is legally still considered to be a part of the shoulder season.

May

Temperatures continue to rise during May, which is the last month of the spring season; nevertheless, they seldom reach intolerable levels. Even if the temperature is on the rise, there is still the possibility that it might rain without any prior notice. The pleasant climate makes it possible for you to participate in a wide variety of outdoor activities, such as going on an exhilarating hike to the top of Gellert Hill to get a bird's-eye view of the city, riding a chairlift to the peak of Buda Hills, or having a relaxing picnic on Margaret Island. All of these activities are wonderful ways to spend time in the great outdoors. You also have the choice of embarking on a bar-hopping excursion among the city's most prominent drinking spots or engaging in a guided tour of the city itself. Both of these activities are available to you. You are more than welcome to join in on any of the city's various spring celebrations, which take place throughout May.

June

Even if the average temperature in June in Budapest is lower than what it is in July and August, you should still prepare for the potential that it could rain while making trip arrangements. The month of June marks the beginning of the summer season in Budapest. Nevertheless, the temperature is generally pretty favorable, which explains why June is the month that sees the biggest number of people coming to see the city. This is because the weather is at its best during this time. At the beginning of summer, a large number of outdoor cafés and bars, including those that are situated on roofs, also open their doors so that customers may unwind while sipping Hungarian beer in the fresh air. There is a myriad of different festivals and events that take place all around the world throughout June. The Danube Carnival and Night at the Museums are two activities that you should not participate in under any circumstances. Throughout June, the city plays home to a vast array of music events that celebrate a wide variety of musical genres.

July

July is without a doubt the month that best depicts summer in its most authentic form, both in terms of the average temperature and the optimistic temperament of individuals who reside in the region, and it is without a doubt the month that. Although a sizeable section of the local population flees the city during winter vacations, the city is buzzing with tourists from all corners of the globe. As part of the city's celebration of the summer season, a broad variety of outdoor performances are scheduled to take place in the evenings during the whole season. In addition, you may consider going to City Park or Margaret Island so that you can listen to live music as you unwind under the night sky there. In addition, the city is host to a large number of events honoring a wide array of topics and topics ranging from street food to beer. In addition, the Hungarian Grand Prix of Formula One takes place during July, offering tourists an extra reason to visit Budapest at this time of year.

August

August in Budapest is relatively comparable to July, with the notable exception of the temperature, which is significantly lower; because of this, August is one of the most popular months for tourists to visit. One of the most significant gatherings is the Sziget Festival, which takes place this month and brings a significant number of visitors to the city. Other events, including the Festival of Folk Arts and the celebration of St. Stephen's Day, are oriented at a more broad audience, in contrast to the Sziget Festival, which is primarily geared toward a younger demographic. Other events include the celebration of St. Stephen's Day and the Festival of Folk Arts. Not only is August a beautiful month for sightseeing due to the abundance of events and festivals that take place throughout the month, but also since the weather is tolerable and the days are long during this time of year.

September

When it comes to visiting Budapest, the month of September is the best option since it falls smack in the center of the city's busy tourist season without being too crowded. Tourists tend to flock in large numbers throughout the summer months of June, July, and August. Even though the great majority of tourists have already left the city, there are still sufficient numbers of locals to prevent the place from giving off the impression that it is utterly dead. The weather in September is sometimes described as having the characteristics of an "Indian summer," which consists of a short period of lower temperatures followed by a few days of higher temperatures. This is the most accurate definition of the weather in September. The month of September in Budapest is home to a multitude of one-of-a-kind festivities and festivals, one of which is the National Gallop Festival, which honors the Hungarian horse history. The arrival of autumn marks the beginning of a whole new season of theatrical performances, some of which include opera and ballet.

October

The first day of autumn in Budapest is celebrated throughout October, and with it comes the city's most beautiful time of year. The leaves of autumn, which have fallen on the ground, make their presence felt across the city by covering every park and every street that is surrounded by trees. There is nothing quite like a peaceful walk around the city of Budapest in October when the weather is not quite as frigid and the sun is not as fierce as it is in other months of the year. October is one of the most popular months for travelers to visit Germany since it is the month in which the Oktoberfest beer festival is held. You should make it a point to attend an incredible Halloween party if you are going to be in the city on the final weekend of the month and you are planning on going.

November

November marks the beginning of the official winter season in Budapest, at which time the days start becoming noticeably darker at an earlier hour and people start breaking out their winter coats. There are still some days in

November that have beautiful fall weather, even though the temperature is starting to drop. Residents have the opportunity to make an early start on their Christmas shopping at the vast majority of night markets and artisan fairs that take place throughout the month. Even though there is often less foot traffic at restaurants and bars with outdoor seating during this month, many establishments continue to remain open for business on days when the weather is pleasant. You are more than welcome to take part in any of the events that are being hosted in honor of All Saints Day on November 1 and the festivities that are being held in honor of St. Martin's Day on November 11 respectively.

December

It is possible to get into the Christmas mood through December in Budapest. If you are interested in performing some present shopping, the city is home to a great number of charming markets that you are free to visit whenever you find the time. At the Christmas markets in Vorosmarty Square, one may find a great number of people, both locals, and tourists alike. These people are shopping for Christmas gifts. During the holiday season, visitors to Budapest may have the opportunity to delight in a variety of traditional seasonal foods and beverages, including mulled wine, roasted chestnuts, kurtas kalas, and the very real possibility of a white Christmas. In addition, there is a profusion of Christmas and New Year's parties that you may attend if you want to have a great time during the holidays.

CHAPTER 6

ACTIVITIES DURING SUMMER

There is something for everyone to enjoy in Budapest, whether one is looking for a location to get their adrenaline dose, a nice price, or a sweet treat to savor during the summer. Budapest has something to offer everyone. During the warm summer months, some of the most popular things to do in the city include indulging in frocks, a classic Hungarian wine spritzer; traveling to one of the biggest music festivals in Europe, and escaping to the tranquil environs of Lake Balaton.

1. At the Gellét Spa, you may feel the exhilaration of riding the wave.

The Gellért Spa is widely recognized as the epitome of Art Nouveau splendor, and the magnificent mosaics that cover its hot pools are the primary reason for the spa's widespread fame. Nevertheless, during May and September, it also has an additional outdoor attraction. The outdoor wave pool in Gellért was the very first of its kind to be constructed anywhere in the world when it initially opened its doors approximately 90 years ago. It is surrounded by a huge area that may be used for sunbathing and resting.

2. On the Liberty Bridge, you may learn more about your freedom.

After the conclusion of each weekend in July, the Liberty Bridge in Budapest, which in Hungarian is referred to as Szabadság HD, is popularly referred to by its nickname, Szabihd.

It is also the moment when the bridge transforms from a highway for heavy traffic between the two sides of Buda and Pest into a public space that is only accessible to pedestrians. This takes place at this time. A session of early morning yoga, a picnic or barbecue with friends, a glass of chilled wine at sunset, and even a party, if that's the type of thing that interests you, are all things that are feasible here. If you're interested in that kind of thing, you can even go to a rave. Check out the events schedule that can be found right here to learn more about what you can expect to take place on the bridge.

3. Get into the spirit of things during the Sziget festival

The Sziget Festival is one of the largest music festivals in Europe, and it takes place throughout August on an island that is located to the north of Budapest's city center. What started in 1993 as a little get-together for folks who liked listening to music has now developed into an event that comprises 1,000 performances spread out over 60 stages over seven days. This event takes place every year in the city of Austin, Texas. People come from all over the globe to be a part of this location because of its pulsating energy, positive vibes, and performances that are on par with the best in the world. Sziget has played host to some notable international acts in recent years, including Rihanna, Sum 41, and Florence + The Machine, to name just a few instances.

4. While in Budapest, be sure to spend some time admiring the public artwork.

The Sznes Város Association is the organization that is responsible for commissioning several murals that can be seen throughout the city. These murals are often multi-story and include vivid colors. This city has a lot to offer to those who like urban and outdoor art, and those people will discover that this city has a lot to offer. It strives to change the common and incorrect impression of graffiti as a method of improving the urban environment for the better via the use of innovative wall paints that make the cityscape more lively. It has completed more than 70 projects at this moment, so it is not hard to discover one of its murals without making an excessive amount of effort. If, on the other hand, you are determined to take control of every aspect of your adventure and not leave anything to chance, District VII is a good place to start your search from.

5. While you're there, take in the view of the city from the other side of the Danube.

Riverboats are not only an essential part of Budapest's public transit system, but they also provide passengers the opportunity to see the city from a unique vantage point and provide a much-needed reprieve from the chaos that can be found on the city's streets. As the boats go through the city's historic core, they pass beneath seven of the city's bridges and provide passengers with stunning views of a broad array of significant monuments along the way. Some of the top locations that fall under this category are Margaret Island, the Hungarian Parliament, Gellért Hill, and the cultural complex that comprises Mupa Budapest (Palace of the Arts), the Béla Bartók National Concert Hall, and the Ludwig Museum.

6. Pedal your way to a green haven in the middle of the metropolis.

The Fellini Culture Pub is a chilled-out summer paradise that may be reached by riding a bicycle along the banks of the Danube and then getting ready to join the establishment. If you are seeking a spot that is magical, one-of-a-kind, and far from the hustle and bustle of the city, then you have found the perfect destination for your needs. It is possible to take in beautiful panoramas of the Danube River, the forested landscape that surrounds it, and even the occasional kayaker while relaxing in the comfort of a colorful deckchair. If the journey has left you feeling peckish, you may satiate your hunger by eating freshly prepared local and international cuisine, washing it down with an icy cold beer, or some frocks while watching a film or live entertainment.

7. If you are looking for a vintage item at a decent price, you should head to the Ecseri Flea Market.

It is strongly suggested that everyone interested in relics, collectibles, vintage products, and antiques make their way to the Ecseri Flea Market, which is situated on the outskirts of the city and is readily accessible by public transportation. At the largest flea market in Budapest, which is a paradise for shoppers looking for relics from the period of communism, you may anticipate finding vintage pictures, military outfits, and a great deal more. In addition, there is a plethora of vintage jewelry, analog cameras, antique watches, and other forms of vintage jewelry to choose from. Taking the bus to go to the market, which will take around forty minutes, is time well spent, especially on Saturdays when the atmosphere at the market is at its most lively.

8. Go wild over the gelato at Fragola's.

Even though there are a lot of retail stores spread out around the city, Fragola's ice cream is, without a question, the most popular and well-liked among the residents, and this is because it serves some of the best flavors available. The ice cream produced by this firm is made from scratch in the company's workshop using only the finest quality ingredients. It is available in a range of 120 different flavors, and the list of available flavors is regularly updated. When you are ready to give in to your want for something sweet and indulge your sense of taste, you have a wide variety of options accessible to you to choose from. You may want to try some cashews and turmeric, or even a spoonful of Hungarian camembert ice cream. Both of these are delectable choices to consider. If you want to get a feel for the region's rich historical heritage, you should have a double scoop of the delicious Hungarian-Jewish flódni cake taste.

9. Escape to Lake Balaton

The largest lake in Central Europe, Lake Balaton is a favorite vacation spot for city inhabitants who wish to escape the oppressive heat of the city for a few days during the summer months. Because it is just a quick train ride away from Budapest, it serves as a convenient weekend destination for residents of the capital city. After beating the heat with a swim and cooling off in its bubbly waters, be sure to sample some of the mouthwatering delights that this historic wine and cheese region in Hungary has to offer. This region is known for its long history of producing cheese and wine. Exploring the stunning coastlines of the Tihany Peninsula might provide you with a wealth of information on the lake that is often referred to as the "Hungarian Sea."

ACTIVITIES DURING SPRING

The cherry trees along Tóth rpád sétány are flowering, the snowdrops are gracing Alcst Arboretum, and the many parks in Budapest are ready for joggers, strollers, and anybody else who is enthusiastic about staying healthy. The season of spring has finally arrived. The following are some of our top recommendations for the springtime, with the hope that by the next season, Budapest will have become a city that is alive, welcoming, and healthy.

1. Take a moment to appreciate the beauty of the snowdrops.

Snowdrops are the first flowers to blossom in the springtime, and the sight of their pure white blooms is certain to put a smile on anyone's face who happens to be in the vicinity at the moment. The Alcst Arboretum can be reached by car in around forty-five minutes from Budapest. It is open every day of the week from ten in the morning until six in the evening, and its plant collection includes seven different species and twenty-four different types of plants. Because the flowers are only in bloom for a brief period, you had best make haste if you want to see them before it is too late to do so.

2. Take a stroll along the Danube's banks.

It doesn't matter whether you're strolling along the Pest embankment or the Buda coastline; the Danube provides the perfect backdrop for any city walk since its surroundings are lovely, secure, and usually important historically. And everything is within easy walking distance from your home's entrance!

3. Let the melody of Bartók's Spring become familiar to your ears.

Beginning on April 2 and continuing through April 18, the massive, multi-arts event series known as Bartók Spring International Arts Weeks will be held digitally for the very first time. The series will include performances from some of the most renowned concert venues in Europe in addition to the very first public performances of brand-new compositions.

4. Take part in the activities that are taking place during the Budapest Spring Festival.

The Budapest Spring Festival will be held from the 9th through the 18th of April this year, and it will be honoring its 40th year with a free event that will take place on an online forum. The event will take place this year. Visual content is at the forefront in 2021 due to the intrinsic nature of digital media, which places it at the forefront of attention. To continue a tradition that dates back forty years, the festival's organizers will plan a special activity or event to take place on each of the days of the celebration. In addition to this, there will be performances that include aspects from the past, the present, and the future.

5. Go out and get some vegan munchies.

The Vegan Weekend Market is slated to make its return on the promenade adjacent to the Allee Mall on April 10-11, after being absent for a considerable amount of time. There is a large selection of wares available for purchase at this market that takes place for two days. These wares include anything from handcrafted creams and soaps to baked foods and cheeses. Get there early and strike up a discussion with the people who manufactured the items to get the inside scoop on how they were produced.

6. Take a look at some classic recordings that are on vinyl.

If the restrictions imposed due to the epidemic are removed on April 11, the Budapest Record Exchange market is set to resume normal business operations. The fair is hosted at the Globe Hall at ELTE on the second Sunday of

every month; thus, music fans may also expect a day in the middle of May for the event. At the booths that are located throughout the venue's perimeter, in addition to selling vinyl records, CDs, and cassette tapes, there will also be music-related merchandise, posters, books, and newspapers available for purchase.
.

7. Take care of yourself by cultivating your garden at home.

Because you will be spending more time indoors, this is the perfect opportunity for you to put your "green fingers" to good use and put your plant-growing skills to the test. The mission of the Budapest-based community group known as Urban Jungle is to assist the city's residents with the growing of their indoor plants. On their Facebook page, they provide users with a plethora of information as well as sound advice. However, the owners are proficient in English and are happy to share their knowledge with others, even if the bulk of the entries are written in Hungarian. Grow some plants in the urban garden you have so that you may make the most of them throughout the months when it is really hot outside.

8. Make it a point to see a show put on by the iamyank Live Ensemble.

Iamyank Live Ensemble was dreamed of as an idea at the Valley of the Arts event that took place in 2017, which took place in 2017. His solo performances and compositions, his world of electronic music, and his happy despair were constants in his persona. On April 17th, iamyank will work inside the comfortable confines of the studio to make textures that will last for a long time but are also susceptible to ongoing change.

9. Stroll along Tóth Árpád sétány

Along the Tóth rpád sétány that runs along the top of Castle Hill, several lovely cherry trees were planted in the 2000s. As a direct consequence of this, this particular promenade has developed into one of the most well-known in the city. As you see Buda come into bloom, be sure to soak in the stunning views that are offered to you by the medieval battlements.

10. Immerse yourself in OFF-Biennale Budapest

The next incarnation of OFF-Biennale Budapest will start in April and will last for a total of five weeks. During that time, participants will be able to take part in artistic activities that are exclusive to the festival. This time around, the focus is going to be on a more select group of projects that are going to be presented in a hybrid digital format. These projects will be considerably more challenging.

11. Decide whatever beautiful plants and flowers you want to use.

On the final weekend of April, Buda Arboretum will play host to the Spring Garden Decorative Plant Exhibition & Fair. The participants will have the option to choose from a variety of back-to-nature design items in addition to the flowers, ornamental plants, and gardening equipment that will be available. There will be a variety of activities, including speeches, displays, and other events, with a focus on the environment.

12. Keep an eye out for antique articles of apparel.

On May 1st, a second outdoor vintage clothing sale will be hosted by the Telep and Judas team on Madách tér in the central business district of the city. If you take your time looking through the piles of shirts and trousers for any antique clothes that are appropriate for the spring, you won't have to worry about the epidemic.

13. Get outdoors and take part in events that are held there.

Even those who would not normally be interested in working out are lured to the city's outdoor gyms as the weather starts to warm up, and those people who already like working out can't wait to get back to it now that the weather has warmed up. Facilities are constantly being increased and renovated all across the city; by the beginning of May, there will also be a new outdoor gym in the Nagyrét neighborhood.

14. Celebrate the first of May

Although it was formerly set aside as the day for the annual parade to commemorate the Communist Party, May Day is currently celebrated as a legal holiday in the United States. Even though it is almost certain that no gatherings will take place, the neighborhood that surrounds City Park has to have an air of relaxation and family friendliness. Of course, this needs to be done while keeping in mind how important it is to retain a social distance.

ACTIVITIES DURING WINTER

There is no getting around the fact that winters in Budapest can be pretty frigid. This is a truth that cannot be overlooked. However, there are also a lot of things to do inside, such as checking out the opera theater, visiting the Christmas markets, and checking out the wrecked pubs, which have the most enjoyable ambiance around this time of year. At this time of year, you should make it a point to attend one of the various spas that Budapest has to offer to revitalize your health, warm up, and relax your muscles.

1. The ice skating rink located inside City Park

It is generally agreed upon that the ice rink located in Budapest's City Park is the most popular spot to go ice skating not just in the surrounding region but also throughout the whole of Europe. Because it is located on the edge of the city park and in front of Vajdahunyad Castle, the rink attracts a large number of skaters throughout the winter season, beginning at the end of November and continuing until the middle of February. The cost of entrance is somewhat less than three euros for children, students, and elderly people; five euros is charged to adults, and eleven euros is charged to families. (3 people total: 2 adults and 1 youngster). The schedule is as follows: 9:00 a.m. to 1:00 p.m., followed by 3:00 p.m. to 9:00 p.m. In case you need any further information, I have included a link to the official website below. This ice rink first opened its doors to the public in the year 1870, making it not only one of the oldest but also one of the biggest in all of Europe.

2. Light spectacular at the basilica

between the winter months, St. Stephen's Basilica puts on a beautiful light show that is even more appealing to the sight than the structure itself. This is especially true if you visit the city between December and January. A light show will take place at the interval every half hour from 4:30 pm until 10:00 pm, and it will take place during those hours. During the Christmas season, visitors get the chance to see some of the most amazing light displays. These performances often recount religious stories and fables via the use of a wide array of bright lights and a variety of sound effects. The brilliant 3D animations that are shown on the front of the building contribute to the creation of an incredible optical illusion.

3. Treat yourself to a relaxing soak in a steamy bath at one of the many spas Budapest has to offer.

A vacation to Budapest in the winter isn't complete without at least one soaks in a steamy thermal bath, which is among the most well-liked activities in the city. Due to the natural springs that are the source of the water for these baths, which have a high concentration of calcium, magnesium, and fluorine, these baths are known to possess remarkable healing and cleansing properties. The price of the ticket, which may range anywhere from 12 to 22 euros depending on the baths and the package, is determined by these factors. The public baths are open every day of the week, starting at nine in the morning and staying open until seven in the evening. The Szechenyi is generally regarded as being among the most luxurious spas in all of

Budapest; it has three indoor and outdoor heated pools. Even if it is snowing outside, the thermal water will always retain its temperature. This allows for a wonderfully enjoyable and beneficial hot-cold experience, which is something you will have to try at some time in your life.

4. Andrassy Avenue and Fashion Street

When you go shopping in Budapest over the winter, you are in for an experience that will live long in the memory. Not only will you be able to wander through the most stylish shops while taking advantage of the largest deals of the year, but you will also be able to soak in the holiday spirit on the streets that have been wonderfully decorated. This will be possible because of the combination of both of these opportunities. Andrassy Avenue and Fashion Street are two of the city's most popular destinations for tourists and shoppers at this time of year. Fashion Street is also one of the city's most popular tourist destinations. The majority of stores in this region keep their doors open from 10 in the morning until 9 in the evening throughout the winter months. In addition, tens of thousands of lights and trees have been strung along the avenue in preparation for the winter holiday season.

While all is going on, on Fashion Street, the promenade that leads to Vorosmarty Square is lined with a wide variety of stores and boutiques of varying sizes. In recent years, the bustling street has developed into a prominent tourist attraction as a direct result of the displays and works that help to make the winter season even more memorable than it already is.

5. During the colder months, the Great Central Market is the place to go to sample some of the traditional dishes served in Hungary. If you find yourself in Budapest during the cooler months of the year, make sure you stop by the NagyVásárcsarnok, sometimes referred to as the Great Market. There are a few standing counters on the second floor that offer traditional Hungarian food as well as wines that are suitable for the current season. When faced with the tantalizing scent of freshly baked strudels and other homemade delicacies, it might be difficult to maintain a firm no. It is my strong recommendation that you make an order for one of the winter specials if you are interested in tasting cuisine that is authentically prepared in the Hungarian style. On a tour of the culinary scene in Budapest, this establishment represents one of the most significant stops.

Grand Central Market is not simply a place to shop since it is always air-conditioned; rather, it is also a place to rest and warm up from the inside out. This is because Grand Central Market is a location. Not hungry? I want you to believe me when I tell you that just taking in the sight of all of the mouthwatering delights that are being offered will induce your stomach to start growling in anticipation. If you are going to Budapest, you should indulge in some of the city's world-famous lángos, which are created right in front of your eyes as you watch. However, it is highly suggested that you consume them in the summertime there.

6. During the winter, you should ride the streetcar at least once.

During December and January, when winter arrives in Budapest, there are special streetcars that are decked up with fairy lights and make their way around the city's most prominent tourist spots. The magnificent beauty of these streetcars' exteriors is what draws people's attention to them. The Fényvillamos is the name given to these streetcars, and in addition to operating as a means of transit, they are also operated as a tourist attraction. In addition, they are a great option for moving about on those frigid nights when there is no one else available to help you out. You can find these illuminated streetcars working along the most prominent routes in Budapest, so if you are interested in stylishly exploring the city, you may take a trip on one of these streetcars.

7. Hungarian State Opera

The gates of the Hungarian State Opera are unlocked during the winter months so that guests may experience a night that is not only warm but also full of music and a nice atmosphere. To combat the dark days of winter, what could be more successful than employing rhythm and expressive art? You are welcome to listen to the music, but in addition to that, you are also welcome to take a tour of the building, which is a historic place and has a lot of fascinating things to look at.

Since it was first built more than 134 years ago, the Hungarian State Opera has not undergone any kind of renovation or change in any form, even though it was completed in the year 1884 and was designed by the prominent architect Miklós Ybl. The spectacular building is now considered a treasured icon of our nation and is frequently utilized in films that make a lot of money.

8. Christmas markets

Even though it takes place in Budapest during the Christmas season, it is still a popular tourist attraction during the rest of the year when it is chilly outside. At the Christmas markets that are hosted in Vorosmarty Square and at St. Stephen's Basilica, guests will have the opportunity to buy mulled wine, Christmas strudel, and other traditional delights, in addition to things that have been created.

Every year, the beginning of November marks the beginning of the holiday season, during which time the markets are open until the beginning of January. They provide an authentic Hungarian Christmas experience that will be ingrained in your memory for the rest of your life and draw a substantial number of travelers from all over the world. They often start their day open at ten in the morning and finish up shop at ten at night.

The market at Vorosmarty Square is not solely one of the oldest in Hungary, but it is also one of the most well-known and visited markets in all of Central Europe. Not only is it located in Hungary, but it is also one of the oldest markets in Central Europe.

9. Don't pass up the chance to attend the Budapest Carnival.

The Budapest Carnival is another event that takes place throughout the winter season. This event is always celebrated in the time between the celebration of the Epiphany and the beginning of Lent, also known as Ash Wednesday. Therefore, if seeing the Farsang is the major reason you want to visit the city, you should schedule your trip for February.

The week preceding the Budapest Carnival is a festival of life, color, and joy that anybody, irrespective of their religious convictions, can take pleasure in and enjoy to some degree. Events that have been practiced for generations, such as Busójás, are held to commemorate the nation's history and culture while also bidding farewell to winter and looking forward to the arrival of spring.

ACTIVITIES DURING AUTUMN

Certain people in the world are unable to see the leaves change color because they are never there at the right time. However, we do have them in Hungary, and one of the most enjoyable ways to get to know them is by taking a stroll around one of the numerous parks that Budapest has to offer. Let's get moving now that we've established both our destination and our plan of action for getting there.

1. Take a stroll smack dab in the heart of the metropolis.

Golden trees can be seen all around the summit of Gellert Hill, which is where we prefer to travel so that we can take in our favorite view of the city. (It is not going to disappoint you at any time during the year.) A huge network of hiking trails can be found winding through the bright seasonal woodlands that may be found in Buda Hills. The spring and the autumn are by far the best times of the year for us to go trekking in that area. This trek will take you from Normafa to Elizabeth Lookout as its endpoint. You might also go up the 495-meter-high Hármashatárhegy and take in the panorama from the vantage point at Guckler Károly. You might also choose to do the journey on foot from Csillebérc to Farkashey.

2. Go for a walk around the various parks.

If you continue down the Danube side, you will eventually arrive at Margaret Island. This little island is home to what is often regarded as Budapest's most beautiful and placid urban park, and it is located in the heart of the city. The citizens of the city make regular excursions to this location throughout the year to bask in the warmth of the sun and breathe in the clean, crisp air.

On the Pest side of the river, you have the choice of going for a walk in Városliget, which is also known as the City Park, Károlyi Kert, or Fuvészkert. (the ELTE Botanical Garden).

3. Stuff your face with great local food and try some of Hungary's world-famous wines while you're there.

Take part in a tour that takes a small group to the Central Market Hall in Budapest. During this trip, you will learn about the culinary culture of the city while eating traditional dishes and drinks (such as lángos, different kinds of meat, and cakes), as well as sipping wines.

4. Visit Kerepesi Cemetery

An air of mystique permeates the grounds of the cemetery on a brisk autumn day, given that it is the last resting place of so many "Magyars" who played important roles in the country's history. Given the size of this park, you must remember to pick up a map at the entrance. In addition, you shouldn't forget to bring your camera with you since there will be a never-ending variety of amazing opportunities to capture photographs of the old sculptures and the shifting colors of the leaves.

5. Atop Castle Hill in Buda, search for the hidden staircases that go down the hill.

A trip around the Buda Castle District is a great way to spend time at any time of the year; but, in the autumn, the district's hidden stairways and alleys that wind their way up the hill look to be especially appealing. Do you need ideas that are accompanied by a particular location? It is possible to locate Gránitlépcs, as well as the steps on Korlát Street and the stairs on Kagyló Street.

6. Have a few sips of hot chocolate.

At the end of the day, do something kind for yourself and indulge in a mug of hot chocolate as a reward for a job well done. Simply said, it is the reward for participating in any activity that takes place outside during the colder months of the year.

7. Satisfy Your Inner (Art) Nerd at One of Budapest's Many Entertaining Museums or Exhibits and Do It While You're Here!

Even if you have gone to some of the most well-known museums in the world, such as the National Museum, the Museum of Fine Arts, or the National, as well as some of the more contemporary museums, such as the Ludwig Museum or the Natural History Museum, there is still a great deal more for you to discover that will pique your curiosity. It is highly recommended that you pay a visit to either the Robert Capa Contemporary Photography Center or the Mai Manó House of Photography to see one of the numerous outstanding photo exhibitions that are hosted at these locations.

If history is more your thing, you absolutely must miss the opportunity to visit the Kiscelli Museum. It will take you by the hand and guide you through the many different times that make up the complicated history of Budapest. Also, if you are interested in seeing some real curiosities, you should go to one of the numerous little museums that Budapest has to offer.

8. Make It a Point to Stop By Some of Your Neighborhood's Arthouse Theaters

When the cooler weather of autumn hits, it's time to go to the movies! On the other hand, you should avoid going to the multiplexes and instead check out one of the amazing independent theaters that Budapest has to offer. Cirkó Gejzr claims that it is the tiniest cinema in all of Europe, whilst Bem Mozi specializes in displaying classic films that you may have either never seen before or could watch again and again. Both theaters are located in Budapest, Hungary. Both of these theaters may be found in the heart of Budapest. All three of these movie theaters, Kino, Toldi, and Mvész, have a great vintage atmosphere, and they all show a diverse range of indie films.

9. Attend a Live Performance

This next autumn will include a lot of spectacular performances that are certain to satisfy music enthusiasts of varying tastes and preferences. Check out the concerts that are taking place at A38, which is a ship that has been transformed into a floating music venue, or at Durer Kert, which is one of the most unique ruin pubs in the city and often hosts live performances by artists from all over the country and the world. Lámpás Bár is the place to go if you want to witness live music, see and support lesser bands, and if you want to watch lesser bands. In this dingy cellar that has a warm and inviting environment, live music is performed almost every night, and the whole experience is consistently pleasurable. You may also go on over to Pótkulcs, Budapest's oldest ruin bar, where they host Irish evenings, worldwide music nights, and regular folk night gatherings in a setting that is authentic to the core.

CHAPTER 7

SAFETY TIPS IN BUDAPEST

If you are contemplating traveling to Budapest on your own, you may find yourself asking, "Is Budapest Safe?" The short answer to your question is "yes," Budapest is, in point of fact, a secure city. There is no need for you to be afraid about your safety if you decide to take a trip to the capital city of Hungary. Nevertheless, you should always be on the watch for potential hazards, just as you do when you visit any other large city in the world. Because of this, you should constantly keep a tight eye on your possessions, steer clear of strolling into dark alleys with tiny passageways, and bear in mind that you can't trust anybody. Your safety is not something that should cause you a significant amount of anxiety while you are in Budapest. On the other hand, even though this is the case, you will find some fundamental suggestions about which components of this page you should concentrate on reading.

Tips when boarding Taxi

Taking a taxi in Budapest is an activity that you should treat with the highest prudence while you are there. While you are there, you should give this activity your whole attention. To scam customers out of more money, drivers often display rude behavior and may even try to take passengers on longer routes than necessary. If you want to take a taxi, the best way to do so is not to get into one on the street, but rather to either have your hotel book one for you or download the Taxify app and make your order using this app. Getting into a taxi on the street is not the easiest way to take a taxi since it is the least convenient method to take a taxi. Read more to learn how to safely run a taxi in Budapest and to get more knowledge about how to operate a taxi.

When you are out and about in the city, the one thing you need to be most cautious about, other than taxis, is becoming a victim of a pickpocket. Always exercise extreme caution and vigilance concerning your belongings, but this is particularly important when you are using public transit, when you are at train or metro stations, or when you are in a marketplace. To restate, this is true for almost every major metropolitan center in the world. This has nothing at all to do with the reality that Budapest is not a safe location for tourists to come to at all.

Is it risky for a woman to stay in a hotel room by herself in Budapest?

It is recommended that any lady who is interested in traveling to Budapest by herself go ahead and make the trip. It is a safe place for female tourists to stay in Budapest who are traveling by themselves. There has not been a single claim made about any kind of assault or harassment that was explicitly intended against women. It should go without saying that the adages "just be aware" and "don't do things you wouldn't do at home" both apply in this situation. Use your common sense. It is not a smart move to go out walking around the streets in the middle of the night by yourself, especially if you are in an unfamiliar area.

Is it risky for a man to stay in a hotel room by himself in Budapest?

Although men are more often the targets of con artists in Budapest, it is recommended that women traveling alone adopt a level of vigilance that is somewhat higher than that recommended for men traveling alone in the city. One of the most common and well-known cons that can be pulled off in Budapest includes ladies enticing guys before they are robbed themselves. When you are out and about in public, you should avoid going to strip clubs and use extreme care if a woman who is all by herself approaches you for whatever reason. You will, in the worst-case scenario, find yourself being held by two strong guys in front of an ATM as you are wedged between them. You should have a delightful and risk-free time in Budapest if you put your newly obtained understanding of this strategy of seduction into action and if you exercise some fundamental good sense.

Some recommendations for your safety
- You should never leave home without a copy of your passport, and you should have this copy stored in a place that is separate from the one in which you keep your original passport.
- Be careful not to bring about an excessive amount of cash. Additionally, under no circumstances should you put your wallet in the pockets of your pants or the rear pocket of your pants. Your best chance for maintaining the safety of your cash is to keep it contained inside a money belt.
- Never ask taxi drivers about their favorite restaurants or bars; they shouldn't be trusted with such information.

- Always take full responsibility for buying your own alcoholic and nonalcoholic drinks and ensuring that they are never out of your line of sight.
- When dealing with somebody you are not acquainted with, you should always use the utmost care.

Places to pay attention to

To state this again, Budapest is a very safe city. Since this is the case, there is no need to be anxious about anything at all. There is one area in the center that requires somewhat more care than the others, and that area is the middle neighborhood. In such a case, you would be in District IX and District VIII, respectively. Despite this, there is no need for alarm since these sites enjoy an exceptionally high level of safety. Just remember to take additional measures after dark, and make every effort to cut down on the amount of time you spend aimlessly wandering about this area. In addition, it is to your benefit to position yourself near the bordering areas, including the Jewish neighborhood and the inner city. Doing so will increase your chances of obtaining favorable outcomes.

Printed in Great Britain
by Amazon